Jeff Allen's Best:
Get the Interview

Other books by Jeffrey G. Allen, J.D., C.P.C.

HOW TO TURN AN INTERVIEW INTO A JOB
(also available on audiocassette)

FINDING THE RIGHT JOB AT MIDLIFE

THE PLACEMENT STRATEGY HANDBOOK

THE EMPLOYEE TERMINATION HANDBOOK

PLACEMENT MANAGEMENT

SURVIVING CORPORATE DOWNSIZING

THE COMPLETE Q&A JOB INTERVIEW BOOK

THE PERFECT JOB REFERENCE

JEFF ALLEN'S BEST: THE RESUME

JEFF ALLEN'S BEST: WIN THE JOB

Jeff Allen's Best: Get the Interview

Jeffrey G. Allen, J.D., C.P.C.

John Wiley & Sons, Inc.

New York • Chichester • Brisbane • Toronto • Singapore

Library of Congress Cataloging-in-Publication Data

Allen, Jeffrey G., 1943—
    Jeff Allen's best: get the interview / Jeffrey G. Allen.
        p.   cm.
    Includes bibliographical references.
    ISBN 0-471-52547-2. ISBN 0-471-52546-4 (pbk.)
    1. Job hunting.   2. Employment interviewing   I. Title.
HF5382.7.A46   1990   90-33827
650.14—dc20   CIP

Printed in the United States of America

90 91   10 9 8 7 6 5 4 3 2 1

*To the countless number of personnel consultants and jobseekers
whose successes fill the pages of this series. May your "best"
instruct and inspire countless others to succeed.*

With appreciation . . .

*To my wife, Bev;
to our daughter, Angela;
to an editor's editor, Mike Hamilton,
   who conceived the series;
and to Louann Werksma,
   who assisted with its research and development.*

You definitely keep me at

"Jeff Allen's best!"

About the Author

Jeffrey G. Allen, J.D., C.P.C., is America's leading placement attorney and Director of the National Placement Law Center in Los Angeles. Experience as a certified placement counselor, personnel manager, and professional negotiator uniquely qualifies him to write this breakthrough three-part series on techniques that will result in getting and winning the maximum number of job interviews.

Mr. Allen is the author of more bestselling books in the career field than anyone else. Among them are *How to Turn an Interview into a Job, Finding the Right Job at Midlife, The Placement Strategy Handbook, Placement Management, The Complete Q&A Job Interview Book,* and *The Perfect Job Reference.* He writes a nationally syndicated column entitled "Placements and the Law," conducts seminars, and is regularly featured in television, radio, and newspaper interviews.

Mr. Allen has been appointed Special Advisor to the American Employment Association, is General Counsel to the California Association of Personnel Consultants, and is nationally recognized as the foremost authority in the specialty of placement law.

Contents

Chapter 8 Miscellaneous Techniques   **121**

Jeff Allen's Best:
Get the Interview

Introduction

Almost 25 years have passed since I began helping people get hired.

I can still feel the thrill of my second placement. My *first* was getting myself hired—as a corporate recruiter. But getting someone *else* hired convinced me a job interview is nothing more than a screen test. An act.

The hiring process will never change. It depends almost completely on the "actor factor." If you get the "casting director's" attention, know your lines, perfect your delivery, and dress for the part, you'll get hired. If you don't, you won't. One big break. No retake.

After my starting role as a corporate recruiter, I spent almost a decade behind a personnel "director's" desk, conducting countless casting calls in hundreds of hiring halls. Interviewing hopeful hirees of every age, stage, and wage, every day (and night—in my sleep). I followed their trials and errors, successes and failures, hits and bombs.

I never viewed that second placement as "beginner's luck." No self-respecting recruiter would. They tell you a lot of reasons why they're successful, but luck isn't among them. After using the techniques in *Jeff Allen's Best*, you'll agree. There's a systematic, consistent, predictable way for anyone to get hired—almost anywhere.

If you look through other "career" books on the shelf, you'll see how "secret" the formula still is. Each author suggests a different approach. Look long enough, and you'll find that half contradict the other half. Some are philosophical, others motivational, and still others personal. Judging by the number of books available on the topic, you'd think everyone who ever got a job is an "expert" on how to get one.

In 1983, Simon & Schuster approached me to write *How to Turn an Interview into a Job*. Its vice-president and senior editor had received a command from the president: "Get that guy!" Nobody knew how the techniques were developed, but they heard how powerfully they worked. I remember the VP's exact words: "We sure can help a lot of people with this book." He was right. We sure did. Probably millions by now. Their success stories are playing on corporate "stages" around the world. They're starring in the roles they do so well. Receiving rave reviews. Writing their own tickets.

Now I specialize in placement law. Thousands of recruiters call and write the National Placement Law Center every year to discuss their placements. Thousands of jobseekers call to report on their successes. "Seconds" become superstars, their careers straight up, their futures assured. Our work continues, as we constantly refine the openers, deliveries, and scripts. But the audience preferences never change. The reaction is always the same: rave reviews. Only more predictably and consistently.

Getting and winning interviews is easy and fun once you know the way. Only the theaters and audiences change—the places and faces—never the reaction. You only need to learn the techniques once, and you're set for life.

I know. You think "background," "qualifications," or "experience" have something to do with getting hired. You're right—not about the *job*, though. About *getting* the job! The director only knows what you show. That's why the actor factor is so "critical."

Through the years, I developed the only measure of jobgetting that counts: the *interview-to-offer ratio*. If you ask enough people, you'll find it averages twelve to one. It takes *twelve* interviews for the average person to get *one* job offer. That means for every person who intuitively knows how to get hired every time (or uses the techniques in this series), some walking wounded is limping into his or her *twenty-fourth* interview. For every two people who get the part on their first screen test, there's someone being carried into his or her *forty-eighth*! Destroyed, not employed.

"Almost chosen" doesn't count. Either you're in or you're

out. When you're hot, you're hot. And when you're *not*—"Don't call us, we'll call you."

After a while, these folks live with a self-fulfilling prophecy: rejection. They might as well just call the interviewer and say, "I'm canceling the interview. Your time is too valuable to waste with me." They're destined to flub their lines from the time the first board claps.

Tragic. Even more tragic when that interview-to-offer ratio will tumble down for *anyone* who'll just use the three books that comprise *Jeff Allen's Best*. The techniques I share for writing your resume, getting an interview, and winning the interview aren't philosophical, motivational, or personal. They're the ones that work every time the curtain goes up. Start ad-libbing, and you'll spend your career making a career out of making a career. If something works, it's in this three-part miniseries. If it doesn't, it's not.

I've long since proven that the best person for the job is someone who can get hired. That's because the people who get the leading roles are the people who are promoted faster, have more self-esteem, and bounce back from the ravages of corporate life faster and higher than anyone else.

So, let's get busy. No more "extra" status. No more understudy roles. No more "bit parts," either. Nuthin' to hit but the heights. Your name in lights. I'll be your coach, manager, and even your agent for a while. Come with me into the winners' world of work. Through the back entrance, in the elevator, up to the office with the star on the door.

The techniques in the three books in this series will get you interviewed and lower the interview-to-offer ratio to around *three* to one. Not because I want them to, not because you need them to, but because they're based on a quarter-century of trial and error. The same way every breakthrough since the dawn of civilization has occurred. Soon you'll see that exploring your career world and discovering yourself in the process is more enlightening, more exciting, and even more enjoyable than all the silver screen scenarios you'll ever watch.

You need training in three specific areas to get hired in a target job—writing your resume, getting interviews, and interviewing to obtain job offers. In this volume, we'll discuss getting interviews.

Chapter

1

Get Ready to Get Interviews

I think it was Sir Isaac Newton who first commented:

You can't fall when you're on the floor.

That's about where the average jobseeker is when it comes to generating interviews. No risk, no reward. No pain, no gain. No try, no fly. That's why the average jobseeker doesn't have a clue about the incredible number of job "openings" anyone can create for themselves.

What *is* a "job" anyway? It's just an artificial, arbitrary arrangement of tasks someone wants done. "Creating" a job requires nothing more than creating a "want"—even a *need*—in that prospect. It's just a self-marketing activity aimed at an untapped market. Do it right, and you create more than a job. You create *the* job you want, and you participate in determining the tasks that comprise it. That participation occurs when you interview before the job is created.

The third book in this series, *Jeff Allen's Best: Win the Job*, prepares you to win those early interviews. But, for now, let's concentrate on something just as important—getting them.

You can't do it without an organized approach, though. A "self-marketing plan" aimed squarely at your target market. A complete plan, too—using direct mail, telemarketing, and personal meetings with "prospects." People call it the "hidden job market." You'll call it the "*obvious* job market!" It's the *applicants* that are hidden. Well—haven't *you* been hiding?

Let's get you penetrating your market. Get ready to get interviews!

6

1. Write a winning resume.

Not just any resume. A *super-resume*. The first book in this three-part series, *Jeff Allen's Best: The Resume*, contains techniques for creating a super-resume—one that gets you hired.

If you missed *The Resume*, read a copy. Your resume is the tool that unlocks 90 percent of all interview doors. It's your "paper profile on a page." It's *you* before you walk through those doors.

The techniques in this book will help you get your resume on the interview pile, but your resume's just got to be super to get from the interview pile to the personnel file.

2. Join the Experience Express Club.

Membership has its placement privileges. Once you develop the right attitude about your experience and how it helps you to contribute, you'll have the confidence you need to get hired time after time. You have to develop a sense of yourself, where you've been and where you're going, before you schedule that first interview.

"How do you get experience if you don't have experience?" I answered that question in *How to Turn an Interview into a Job*:

> That question is heard more by personnel consultants than any other. It is also the most tragic statement of all in the negativism that afflicts so many people seeking employment. The tragedy is that it is based upon the false premise that you don't *have* experience. In fact, *everyone* who is the same age has the same amount of experience. It's just that some people have more in certain areas than others. The correct question then is: "How do you get experience you can put on a resume or application, and use in an interview?" Now you're talking!
>
> Most people would agree that the practice of law or medicine requires a high degree of knowledge and skill. However, a

practicing lawyer or doctor spends less than 10 percent of professional time in anything that requires independent judgment. Even in these technical professions, over 90 percent is common sense and general knowledge. The less skilled the occupation, the lower the percentage of independent judgment required. That is the reason automation continues to displace millions of people every year.

The saying "He doesn't have ten years' experience, he has one year's experience ten times" is far closer to reality. All that matters is acquiring the maximum 10 percent knowledge that makes one job different from another. It is this phenomenon that causes a subordinate to fear a promotion to the boss's job. Once it occurs, the "bends" subside quickly. It is nothing more than an optical illusion; the view is always different from the outside looking in.

For you, the message is clear: Experience *is* the best teacher ... so good that you need only a little bit. This reality applies whether you are starting your first job or your last. At least 90 percent is life experience.

... *Any* experience you can parlay is what you need to qualify for your Experience Express card.

The club motto is:

EXPERIENCE IS NOT WHAT YOU'VE DONE,
IT'S WHAT YOU DO WITH WHAT YOU'VE DONE.

Leave home with the card, and you'll return with offers ... carte blanche![1]

Pay your membership dues so you can flash your card. Experience will also teach you to believe in your own value. Your confidence will be apparent in your pre-interview communication. It's essential for setting up interviews.

3. Assess your career.

If you followed *Jeff Allen's Best: The Resume*, you completed a thorough career assessment. It begins with a *job inventory*, which is a detailed, written summary—one page for each job—of the work you did and the results you've accomplished.

The next step is to decide what you liked doing, and what you did best. They're invariably the same because:

**We do best what we like most, and
we like most what we do best.**

We earn more when we find this combination, too. Then . . .

4. Give yourself a career makeover.

Ask yourself why you are looking for another job. Is your present job emotionally satisfying or financially rewarding? Why not?

Are you antsy because you're on a self-imposed timetable? Is someone else's opinion influencing you? Can you improve your present job, salary, or future with the company? How? What is the risk? What is your contingency plan?

If you decide to make a move, make sure you make the right one for you—one that will take you closer to your ultimate goal.

5. Get additional training.

Making the right move might require you to increase your qualifications. Perhaps you need specialized training. Take a few courses or workshops to bring up your skills. You might even enroll in a program that leads to a marketable degree.

6. Move from generalist to specialist.

I wrote *Surviving Corporate Downsizing* for those who wanted employment and enjoyment during corporate quakes, shakes, and breaks. It contains an entire chapter about the benefits of specialization and how to reap them without leaving your desk.

Generalists no longer have the most job security. Although their experience remains "transferable," they are being displaced more rapidly as their administrative functions are eliminated, combined, or automated.

Since there's so much competition, generalist resumes result in miles and miles of piles. The only generalists hired are the ones who pile and file them. Today, you have to specialize. Let's review some critical elements on the subject of specialization from *Surviving Corporate Downsizing*:

Aside from increasing your value to your employer, you'll also find that specializing increases your self-worth. We all equate who we are with what we do. . . . [R]emember that specializing should be nothing more than *concentrating on doing what you like to do*. That's why specialists are usually more satisfied with their jobs. It's also why they tend to be more effective than their generalist counterparts.

As I mentioned in the Introduction, I started out as a recruiter. Next I became a personnel manager, then an attorney, then developed the specialty of placement law, and then became an author in the career field. I'm amused when people comment that I "chose" a good legal specialty. I'd like to take the credit for it, but the fact is I couldn't get a job when I graduated from college. Being a commissioned recruiter (oh, excuse me, "management consultant") was my only alternative to selling vacuum cleaners door to door.

Nevertheless, it was a start to a specialty. *Every* job is a start to a specialty! With it, I was able to write a resume to enclose with my cover letter. Then came a personnel job, then another, and another . . . each building on the one before. Then came night law school, a law clerk job, a law degree, the bar exam, private practice, appointment as trade association counsel, a call from Simon & Schuster [then John Wiley & Sons], bestsellers, tapes, tours, etc.

How many "careers" did I have? One! It's called "life." A "job" is just a specific type of life experience; a "career" is just a cluster of jobs.

Look at *any* successful person and you'll find someone who has realized that *each job should be connected to the next.*

It's like those dot-to-dot games, with you pursuing your "career" in the completed picture. That's why abrupt "career changes" destroy so many potential superstars. They draw the lines out of sequence and, even if they try to erase or retrace them, they never really complete the picture. You see, the career game is timed . . . lifetimed. It's irreversible.

Specializing is nothing more than applying one of the more basic success principles:

If you want to be successful, you either have to do your job better than everyone else, or do something everyone else isn't doing.[2]

7. Choose an objective.

Once you've completed the career assessment and makeover, you're ready to select an objective. This includes the kind of job you want, and where you want to do it. It includes items like office environment, employee benefits, salary, potential, security—going from *requirements* to *preferences*—in order of importance.

Your career objective should reflect both personal and professional requirements. Here's an example:

Career Objective

Position Title: Manager, New Business Development; reporting to Director of Marketing or similar.

Organization Type: Service-oriented business (i.e., insurance, financial services, etc.) with minimum 1,000 employees and $30 million per year in revenues. Industry leader and innovator.

Location: Mid-sized metropolitan area in Northeast, Northwest, or Great Lakes Region.

Requirements:

- Salary $65–75K.
- Employer-paid benefits, including medical, dental, disability, and life insurance.

- Environment that encourages creativity and innovation. Matrix organization with less management involvement and more staff support of new product development.
- Incentive and reward based on productivity and performance.
- Less than 25 percent travel.

Preferences:

- Minimum staff of three, including a market researcher, program analyst, and administrator.
- Sign-on bonus of at least $5,000.
- Reimbursement of relocation expenses, including commission on sale of house and interim living expenses.
- On-site day care or comparable assistance program.
- Profit-sharing, pension, or other savings plan.
- Spacious office with a view.

8. Target your search.

There are 100 million jobs in America, and you only need one. Narrow your search to the industry or area of the country that offers the most potential. You'll save yourself time and money if you decide in advance what that means to you.

Make a list of possible employers, then . . .

9. Search your target.

If you're aiming at a public company, call and request a copy of its annual report. If a private company is your target, request a brochure or catalog that will tell you more about its profile, programs, and products.

Then there's the public library, and such reference materials as:

Business Periodicals Index (H. W. Wilson Company)
Dictionary of Occupational Titles

Directory of Corporate Affiliations

Directory of Executive Recruiters

Dun and Bradstreet's Million-Dollar Directory

F&S Index of Corporations and Industries

Forbes: Annual Report of American Business

Forbes 500s

Fortune 500

MacRae's Blue Book

Moody's Manuals

Moody's News Reports

Standard Directory of Advertisers

Standard & Poor's Corporation Records

Standard & Poor's Register of Corporations, Directors, and Executives

Thomas Register of American Manufacturers

U.S. Bureau of Labor Statistics: Area Wage Surveys

U.S. Industrial Product Directory

Value Line Investment Surveys

Wall Street Journal Index

100 Best Companies to Work for in America

Just be sure you don't spend all your time *researching* instead of *searching*. Many of these references are designed for the financial investor, and you often have to read between the lines to come up with something useful for you. Because library labor can be lengthy . . .

10. Become a telephoner.

Sales, marketing, customer service, public relations, and personnel departments are the best sources of information. These are staff functions accustomed to telephone inquiries.

Even receptionists or switchboard operators can be extremely helpful if they're not too busy, since their jobs are often the nerve center through which information flows. Because they regularly deal with the public, they're accustomed to fielding questions. Establish rapport with these individuals, and if they don't have the answers to your questions, they'll readily route you to someone who does.

Here are some questions you can ask to obtain general company information:

1. Where is the business headquartered?
2. Who owns the business?
3. How many facilities does the business have?
4. What divisions does the business have?
5. How many employees does the business have?
6. What are the main products or services of the business?
7. What markets does the business serve?
8. What are the new products or services of the business?
9. What are the annual sales of the business?
10. How long has the business been in operation?

You can get even more specific, and ask for the department where you'd like to work. You may find yourself talking to someone who will eventually interview you, so be careful to remain professional, polite—and anonymous. Don't talk about yourself. Learn about the employer.

Instead of asking direct questions about job *openings*, make general inquiries about job *opportunities* and the nature of the operation. If your information-gathering call becomes a job-hunting call, you will be transferred to the human resources department where you'll get the standard, "Send a resume and we'll review it" line.

Later, armed with the intelligence gathered from your telephone sleuthing, you will be prepared to get—and win—an interview.

11. Make jobsearch research a regular habit.

Gathering intelligence on target employers is easier if you do it on a regular basis. Read trade publications, scan business publications and newspaper sections, make contacts at meetings, and generally develop your contacts *all the time.*

Don't regard the job search as something you do until you accept a new job. Keep an eye on your career horizon and you'll never be blown away when the winds shift.

12. Use an answering machine for your residence telephone.

This is a critical step. If you're looking while still employed (Isn't everyone?), it can be uncomfortable—and risky—to take calls at work.

If your home telephone is answered by a family member, no matter how professional his or her answer, the wrong impression is conveyed. And if *you* answer the telephone at home during the day—forget it! That telephone call will telegraph the message: "Unemployed and not doing much about it" (even if you are). You might come home to a series of dial tones.

There's another reason that you don't want to pick up the phone when you're not ready. In his best-selling book *Power! How to Get It, How to Use It,* Michael Korda wrote: "The person who receives a telephone call is always in an inferior position of power to the person who placed it."[3]

The answering machine gives you an edge. It's professional, and lets you get back to the employer when *you're* prepared to talk. You won't get caught off guard with a telephone call from one of 50 companies that received your resumes. ("W-w-w-what's your name? *What* company? N-n-n-o, he ran away from home.")

Include your home number only, designated as a "message number" on your resume. If you use an answering device with remote capability, return the calls the same day. Otherwise, early the next day is acceptable. The message should be recorded in your own voice, and state pleasantly:

> "Hello! This is (first name) (last name). I regret that I'm unable to answer your call at this time. However, if you leave your name, number, and a brief message at the tone, I'll return your call as soon as possible. Thank you for calling."

13. Don't substitute an answering service for an answering machine.

Unlike answering services, machines don't yakety yak, don't talk back, and don't throw out the papers in the trash. That helps you get more spendin' cash.

Busy, time-conscious people have learned to appreciate answering machines. They're the fastest, most reliable, most consistent way to leave a message. Unlike an answering service, a machine is not subject to human error, hearing loss, or frustration. It answers just the way it should, when it should. If it doesn't, it can be replaced by another machine!

Answering services can be extremely rude, inefficient, and far more expensive than the best machine. They also give the impression that you're a professional job jumper.

14. Order personal stationery.

Quality, conservative letterhead will give a good impression. Order it from a stationery printer, not an instant one. Use white or ivory paper, at least 24-pound weight, with a raised, conservative typeface in black ink.

As I wrote in *Jeff Allen's Best: The Resume*:

> Jobgetting typefaces are the more conservative styles, such as Times Roman, Century Schoolbook, and Palatino. These are

readable, available, and acceptable. They are all serif types
..., which are considered to be traditional and businesslike.[4]

I recommend that you order a supply of 8 1/2 x 11-inch
stationery and No. 10 business envelopes imprinted with your
address in the upper left-hand corner. This is fine for your resume
and also for letters. If you'd like to use monarch size stationery
(7 1/4 x 10 1/2 inches) for thank-you notes and cover letters, go
right ahead. It's your money. But it isn't necessary.

15. Complete a sample job application.

You can call any employer and request an application. Then look
up all the old addresses and phone numbers you'll need so that
you can complete it. That way you'll be prepared with answers
to questions about everything from your financial status to
traffic violations.

Once you've gathered the information, type it neatly and
make 20 clean copies. Keep a few in your briefcase for interviews.
It will save time—you'll only have to transpose the information
onto their form.

You should also give your sample completed application to
job references (see Chapter 4). Your resume should also be given
to coach them on the details of your background. When they're
knowledgeable, they'll help you end those interesting interviews
with outstanding offers.

16. Consider moving up instead of out.

As I told millions of career catatonics in *Surviving Corporate
Downsizing*, people tend to forget that every company—even the
one they're working for—is a mini-job market.

[Employers] spend tens of thousands of dollars on ads, campus recruiting, placement fees, hire-on bonuses, and inflated
starting salaries when they've already hired, trained, and

favorably evaluated the best candidates for jobs. Even when they recognize the value of existing employees, they downsize fantasize that someone will come along who'll say magic words, then wave the magic wand. During a downsize, they're particularly susceptible to hiring magicians.

In one sense, marketing to your employer is easier than looking for a job elsewhere. After all, you already know where the bodies are buried. You know the weaknesses in management, the idiosyncrasies of supervisors, the coworkers who sleepwalk through their work, and the jobs that never get done. You also know the corporate culture, consisting of everything from its value system to the buzz words that form its language. In marketing terms, you know the audience.

Marketing to your employer can also be more difficult. For one thing, you're both the goods and the salesperson. This makes it difficult for you to appear objective. For another, you're a known quantity. When you were hired, you were an unread book with an intriguing cover. Now, you've been read many times, and the critics have written their reviews. They're never raves.[5]

Considering this, moving up is less expensive and risky than moving out. To position yourself for a promotion . . .

17. Give yourself a moveup checkup.

Do this even if you've ruled out a promotion (or it's been ruled out for you). Analyze how you appear to others. Your looks, attitude, and behavior must all be considered to get you ready for your next move. Here are more tips from *Surviving Corporate Downsizing*:

> The way you look is the single most important factor in your marketing strategy. You can be the most valuable employee in the organization and have the best personality, but if you don't appear that way to those who matter, you're just working harder, not smarter. After all, if you're gonna stay with the circus, you've gotta look like a clown.

Improving your looks is much easier and much more fun than improving your credentials or disposition. The problem most people have is that grooming and dressing are habits that establish themselves without conscious effort.

A "moveup checkup" can be a painful experience, but be tough on yourself. Look at that "cover" you sell at work in a full-length mirror . . .

Why do you think aspiring actors, politicians, lawyers, and people in every occupation look like the people at the top? Why do you think they're called "role models"? If you follow their lead, you'll succeed. Actors have known the rule for centuries:

Look the part,
and the part plays itself.[6]

Once you've internalized this rule, run through the following checklist with brutal honesty:

❑ **HAIR**

Make sure it's always clean and the right style for the position. With very few exceptions, neat, conservative, natural-looking hair is the rule. Only wear new-wave hairstyles if the people at the top do. Advise your hair designer to use restraint.

Men, keep the sideburns trimmed and the back of the neck shaved between haircuts. Avoid goose grease, chicken fat, and attempts to disguise balding. Bald is believable—it's real.

❑ **FACE**

Women

Observe the makeup style and color used by top female office holders in the company and follow it. Pay seasonal visits to department store makeup counters. Buy quality makeup for your interview screen test. Keep your look fresh but understated.

Men

Only wear a beard or mustache if the top executives do. Keep an electric shaver in your desk drawer and use it when necessary.

❑ **HANDS**

In some companies, men manicure their nails and use clear nail polish. Check this out. Successful women maintain a certain nail length and color, too.

❑ **WARDROBE**

There are shelves of books on how to dress. The best are still *John Molloy's New Dress for Success* and *The Woman's Dress for Success Book.*[7] Wardrobe consultants in better stores will advise on the right colors and styles for you, too. Before you follow their advice, just make sure it's right for your target job. Observe and imitate.

❑ **HEIGHT AND WEIGHT**

If you're above average height, there's not much you can do except celebrate if you're a man. Wear flats if you're a woman.

If you're a shorter-than-average man, you can call Richlee Shoe Company at 1-800-343-3810 (1-301-663-5111 in Maryland) and request their catalog of elevator shoes. Their selection ranges from running shoes to quality wingtips, and you'll gain two inches in height without anyone knowing your secret.

If you're a shorter-than-average woman, there is a wide range of shoe styles and heel heights to help you get up there eyeball to eyeball.

As for weight, you already know what's acceptable and should know how to get there.

A crash diet will deplete your reserves when you need them most, so eat sensibly: fish, poultry, and lean meat; fruits, vegetables, and whole grains instead of processed foods made with refined sugar, enriched flour, and saturated fat. Read labels. It's motivation enough to diet.

Exercise will improve your outward appearance more than dieting, and will improve stamina, energy, and attitude as well. You don't have to join a gym. Try walking. A five-mile morning walk does the trick for Buck Rodgers, CEO of IBM (and for me).

These physical improvements, both inward and outward, coupled with your renewed sense of career purpose, will have your high-octane fueled, tuned, jobgetting engine revving and ready to go.

18. How to get interviews when you're unemployed.

Don't tell anyone.

Everybody wants what someone else has. That's why you see a few actors on the screen constantly while the rest can't get a screen test. Directors—including the ones that hire people like you—don't take chances. They don't really care what they pay, either. They just want somebody in *demand*.

This life makes it harder for you to even look for a job when you don't have one, too. Since your secret job is finding the next one, organize your search like you would organize any job. Strive for maximum productivity. Get up every morning and dress as if you were going to work (you are), even if you don't have appointments that day. As I said in *How to Turn an Interview into a Job*:

> There is a tendency, particularly when you have not been eating regularly, to set up interviews in a random manner. The result is a wide variance in your metabolic rate, attention span, and response time.
>
> If you were laid off or fired from your last job, a measured approach to interview scheduling is the only way to get you emotionally back on the track. It is a psychological fact that physical activity is the best cure for depression. Make interviewing your job until a better one comes along.
>
> The winners in sports and almost every other human endeavor know that consistency is what gives them the edge. You are exercising your interviewing muscles and are jogging

...not running...not walking. If you are out of work, set your goal at one interview around 9:00 A.M. and one interview around 2:00 P.M. Neither should last more than two hours.

Use a calendar with room for daily entries, and set up appointments compulsively: two a day. Soon, you'll have rhythm. It will do wonders for your self-confidence.[9]

If you find yourself in a day without interviews, feel very guilty. You blew it. Spend that day compulsively on the telephone setting up interviews. (More on telephone technique in Chapter 2.) Don't turn on the television. You can't afford a babysitter. Scan (rhymes with "fan") the morning newspaper and whatever publications you need to keep you ahead of what's happening in the job market. Then get on the phone. Get appointments. Get *going*!

19. How to look when you're still employed.

Are you employed and looking? I hope so. An ongoing job search is fun and gives you a low-risk, common-sense way to evaluate your present position against what's available. It's jobsearch research that gives you ammunition for effective negotiations with your present employer, or an edge if you have to leave in a hurry.

It's easier to get a loan when you've got one, and it's easier to get a job when you've got one, too. You communicate confidently because you're financially and emotionally secure. These important differences can turn your current job into a springboard to a better job any time.

While looking for a job really is a full-time job, you can't sacrifice what you have for what you want. When you get a positive response, you run the risk of becoming an "interviewaholic." This jeopardizes your present position by distracting you from your primary task of earning a living *and* can alert your current employer to your clandestine activities. (They'll wonder why you're smiling.)

So guard against conveying your plans—consciously or unconsciously—to your boss and coworkers. It can cause you to exit before you're ready to go. This is how to prevent that from happening:

- Be careful in making calls. Do it after hours unless you have complete privacy in your office.

- Avoid giving search signals. Secretaries, switchboard operators, and mailroom clerks are usually the first to notice the symptoms (cryptic phone calls, frequent "doctor appointments," "Personal and Confidential" envelopes, etc.).

- If you let prospective employers know you're "being paid to do a job," and it would be "inappropriate" for you to take company time to conduct personal business, they'll be favorably impressed. (Nobody talks like that anymore.) You have a lot of "responsibilities" to your present employer, and you won't let anything interfere with your "effectiveness." (They'll be mentally writing out your sign-on bonus check.) Your integrity will win you special treatment in scheduling interviews before or after hours and weekends.

- Leave your home phone number for return calls and make sure your answering machine is on. If your family uses the telephone a great deal, install a second line for your job calls. It's an investment that costs less than parking your car for a single interview in an office building.

20. Schedule interviews no more than two hours apart.

As I said in *How to Turn an Interview into a Job*, this two-hour scheduling is crucial for two reasons:

1. You want it to appear as though you have another commitment. If you don't, make one. People always

want what they can't have, and you're starting to run out of gas anyway.

2. It helps you to avoid eating a meal with someone in the hiring process. There is so much that can go wrong in terms of personal mannerisms, offhanded remarks, eating or drinking habits, and etiquette, that the "businessman's special" can be you! For higher-level positions, this may be unavoidable, so attempt to ask discreetly. If it is merely an invitation and not a requirement, graciously decline. You don't want to sacrifice a job for a meal.[10]

Ready to Go

If you followed these rules, you're ready to get interviews. Chapter 2 shows you how to turn your telephone into an automatic placement machine.

Chapter

2

Telephone Techniques

The telephone revolutionized communication, but "bent" it too. It can distort a message for better or worse.

It's easier to hang up on a voice than to shut the door on a face. Yet, telemarketing operations rack up billions of dollars in sales annually. They play the numbers, but they're systems players. You can self-telemarket just as systematically.

While it's easier to be misinterpreted on the telephone than in person, it's also easier to avoid being prejudged on physical appearance, mannerisms, and style of dress.

Telephone calls can be interruptions, intrusions, and instant insults. To be effective when you call, you have to help your listener change "concentration channels" from personal interaction or thoughts to your voice.

Learn to self-telemarket, and Ma Bell can be your matronly matchmaker. Let's see how.

21. Perfect your delivery.

Do you really know how you sound to others on the phone? Do you come across assertively, confidently, and professionally? Do you sound interesting? Would *you* hire you? If you don't know, find out. Before you talk to others, pick up the handset and talk to yourself.

That answering machine I recommended serves a dual purpose. Use it to perfect your delivery. Prepare a script based on the suggestions that follow for the "deep breath phone call" or the "consultant phone call." Then sit down at another telephone (in a phone booth if you have to), call yourself up, and record your conversation. It's helpful to have a friend waiting for your call to act as an interviewer.

Either way, be sure the call is recorded on your machine. When you play back your recording, evaluate the content and style.

Let's talk about content first. Are your words appropriate to your audience? Trade "buzzwords" and language unique to your field should be saved for the departmental hiring authority; keep your conversations with human resourcers simple. If they get confused, they won't invite you for an interview. They don't want hirees to know they're over their heads.

Make sure your words carry authority and authenticity. Convey to the listener that you know what you're talking about without reading a telemarketing script. Don't bang your gums on the interviewer's drums. Motormouths get tired before they're hired.

Make sure you sound *clear*. Don't slur. Eliminate extra words and phrases. Get rid of "Ah," "y'know," "like," and pregnant pauses.

Under pressure, some people skip back to repetitive openers like a broken record. If you find yourself saying, "As I said," "Needless to say," or "Given this," stop. It's a verbal tick that's as annoying to hear as a facial one is to watch.

Do you talk too fast to be understood? Slow down. Is your speech already slow enough to start a sleep-walking staffer snoring? Discipline yourself to deliver with an even tone and moderate pace.

Practice, record, listen, then practice again until you've eliminated any speech patterns that steer you away from clear, direct, one-to-one communication.

22. Attach a mirror to your telephone.

Ever catch yourself in a mirror with a glum look, sagging shoulders? You smiled and straightened up real fast, didn't you?

A negative expression and poor posture reveal themselves in your voice. Smile! Your positive personality will be telegraphed naturally.

In Chapter 1, I mentioned dressing for work every day, even if you're not employed. Sit down at the telephone to make calls looking your business best, too. When you see that confident, polished professional smiling back at you from the mirror, the satellite will pick up your self-assured signals and beam them right to the hiring authority. You're in!

23. Avoid rejection shock.

Jobseeking can be a "No" business. But you have to avoid internalizing "rejection shock." This insidious disease attacks millions. A rapid heartbeat when talking with prospective employers is the major symptom.

If you make a telephone call and get a "no interest" response to your best interview delivery, don't hang up and connect with the next caller while still experiencing "No woe." As Maxwell Maltz noted in *Psycho-Cybernetics*:

> A human being always acts and feels and performs in accordance with what he imagines to be true about himself and his environment. This is a basic and fundamental law of mind. It is the way we are built.[11]

This is the scientific explanation behind the need to "think positively." Each time you pick up the telephone, it's a new beginning—a chance for something better. You have to *think* you're a winner to *be* a winner. If you contract rejection shock, each phone call will become a self-fulfilling prophecy—rejection.

If necessary, just keep reminding yourself that there are 100 million jobs out there—and you only need one of them. The right one, of course.

24. Dial a "deep breath telephone call."

Every person who believes "Don't call us, we'll call you," is still waiting for the call. There is only one way to break that syndrome. Take a deep breath, and call the interviewer. These are the instructions I gave telephobic jobseekers in *How to Turn an Interview into a Job*:

> I know you think the interviewer will be angry at you, and you therefore will not be hired. It's like calling your first blind date. But the reality is that you are just replaying old memories. In fact, the average interviewer who is hiring is so busy trying to place job orders, run advertisements, review resumes, arrange for interviews, interview, verify employment data, check references, rationalize why the position hasn't been filled, and justify exceeding the hiring budget, that there is not *time* to be angry.
>
> Of course, there are an infinite number of variables in phone conversations, and you might be calling a supervisor directly. However, the illustration that follows will give you an idea of how to position yourself. The words may vary, but your *attitude* shouldn't.
>
> Now . . . sitting comfortably at your desk . . . take a deep breath . . . exhale slowly . . . and place the call.
>
> **Receptionist:** Good Morning. Company X.
>
> **You:** Hi. Mr. (last name) please. This is (first name) (last name) calling.
>
> **Receptionist:** May I tell him what this is regarding?
>
> **You:** (First name) asked me for background information regarding the (title) position.
>
> **Receptionist:** Have you sent us a resume?
>
> **You:** Yes, and I need to fill him in on a couple of points.
>
> **Receptionist:** Just a moment, please. I'll ring . . . Sorry, the line is busy. Can I take your number?

You: No, I'm sorry . . . I'll be out of the office. I'd better wait.

Receptionist: It might be a while.

You: I'll wait, thanks.

Receptionist: I can ring now.

Interviewer: (First name) (last name).

You: Hi, Mr. (last name). This is (first name) (last name). I've been hoping to hear from you to discuss the (title) position.

Interviewer: I'm sorry, we've been just deluged with responses. You're still being considered and we hope to let you know within a week or so.

You: I know how hectic things must be. I'm under a bit of pressure myself, and it looks like I'll have to make a decision soon. The (title) position sounds like a great opportunity, and I'd really like to discuss it personally as soon as possible.

Interviewer: Hang on a minute. . . Oh, here's your resume. . . . When did you leave your last employer?

You: I'm sorry, but I'm just about to leave for an appointment. I'd really like to meet you soon. How about tomorrow morning at 8:00?

Interviewer: I can see you at 9:30.

You: I'll rearrange my schedule. I'm looking forward to meeting you!

Interviewer: Thank you, see you then.

You: Goodbye.

Interviewer: Goodbye.

You have been direct, time-conscious, businesslike, and *affirmative.* You have played out your poker hand in a measured way, and have gathered a few chips. The trick is to get the interviewer on the phone, and you off the phone into his office.

Although I have represented the interviewer as being in the personnel department rather than in the department where you will actually be working, the principles are exactly the same. Generally, the higher the job, the higher the level of the person you can safely contact. The risk is that you will alienate the personnel department, so proceed with caution. Personnel interviewers screen rather than hire. What you don't know can *screen* you, but your ultimate goal is to reach the decision maker![12]

25. Connect with the "consultant telephone call."

There's another telephone technique that takes a bit more preparation and strategy than the deep breath phone call. It's one I recommended in *Finding the Right Job at Midlife*. I called it "the midlifer's key to obtaining as many interviews as possible," but any savvy seeker can use this strategy to get interviews—and offers.

> The key to obtaining interviews is to view the appointment as an end in itself, not just a means to an end. If you do, you will be overcoming the self-imposed obstacles in your way. . . .
>
> Personal contacts (business associates, former supervisors and co-workers, and friends) are the primary networking source to obtain interviews. . . . Although the number of contacts would seem to increase with age, this is not the case for the two largest segments of the middle-age jobseeking population: Those who haven't changed jobs recently and those who are reentering the job market after an extended absence. If you're one of them, your easiest entry to a job interview—and especially to the unadvertised jobs—is to market yourself as a "consultant."
>
> Before you can join the "advice squad," however, bear in mind those factors that are the hallmark of the consultant image:
>
> • An age of 40 to 70. (Increasingly, this span is widening to include younger—and older—consultants.)

- A judicious look on your face (when you're not smiling, of course).
- An ultra-conservative dress or suit.
- An ability to pronounce at least 20 of the latest "buzzwords" in your field (trade publications are the best place to learn them).
- A brochure about your expertise and services (in addition to a . . . resume).
- A business card.
- A local business license (if required).[13]

Making an initial consulting appointment is easy because there is no risk or expense to the client. And, if you're hired, your services can cost them less and save them more than the "experts" already on the payroll.

According to the United States Chamber of Commerce, more than one-third of a typical business payroll is devoted to administration alone: recordkeeping, bookkeeping, government reporting, cash-flow management, payroll taxes, paid holidays, paid vacations, paid sick leave, paid insurance, etc.

"Independent contractors" start out with favored status because they save a company payroll taxes, payroll recordkeeping time, and a lot of other time and money. They don't run to the Equal Employment Opportunity Commission or other government agencies with medical condition, physical handicap, sex, or age discrimination complaints. They don't run up costs for group medical benefits, workers' compensation, or disability claims, either. They get paid for what they do—often a percentage of savings or profits they directly create—and their earnings are reported on a simple IRS Form 1099. They're responsible for reporting their own income and paying their own taxes. And they're usually regarded as miracle workers who've saved the day—even if they only do what employees have been telling management to do all along.

This arrangement is not available for hourly (nonexempt) jobs unless you are engaged in the activity on a freelance basis, and various restrictions exist. If you're in this category, call your state labor department to find out whether you're eligible.

Making your first consulting appointment is as easy as picking up the *Yellow Pages*. (Get a copy of the *Business-to-Business Yellow Pages* if it's available in your market.) With your appointment calendar open, begin with the As.

As a consultant, it is easier for you to bypass personnel and go straight to the hiring authority than if you are a prospective employee. It's an accepted practice for consultants to discuss projects directly with those responsible for them. As I further explained in *Finding the Right Job at Midlife*:

> A competent advisor listens well, probes, asks questions, uses the same vocabulary as the client, and avoids "shooting from the lip." The appointment is an *end in itself*. The call is the means. It's usually about five minutes in length. Any longer will reduce the chances of a personal meeting. You're interviewing, not arranging, if the conversation lingers. More investigation is needed for an interview. This is how the voice of experience sounds:

Receptionist: Good Morning, Company X.

You: Hi. What's the name of your Director of Finance?

> [The research methods I suggested in Chapter 1 can help you determine in advance the person you should speak to; then you can make it appear to the receptionist that you're already known to him or her.]

Receptionist: We don't have a Director of Finance. Would you like to speak to our Chief Accountant?

You: Yes, please. Who is it?

Receptionist: Gail Davis is her name.

You: Thank you.

Receptionist: One moment please, I'll ring . . .

Secretary: Accounting. May I help you?

You: Hi. Ms. Davis, please.

Secretary: May I tell her who's calling?

You: (First name) (last name).

Secretary: May I tell her what it's regarding?

You: Sure. I wanted to speak to her about your cost control system.

Secretary: Is there something I can help you with?

You: No, I'm sorry. I really must speak with Gail.

Secretary: Just a moment . . . I'll see if she's available.

Supervisor: Gail Davis.

You: Hi, Gail. My name is (first name) (last name). I'm a consultant in the finance area, and would like to discuss how I might assist with improving your cost control system.

Supervisor: Our system works fine. Well . . . there are a few things that could use improvement.

You: I'm really familiar with this, and have been very successful in reducing costs with clients. What areas do you see as needing improvements?

Supervisor: Inventory control has really become a problem. We're just unable to keep track of our costs!

You: Your costs? Why?

Supervisor: Well, our production control group has not been following up on status reports.

You: An objective appraisal can often help to straighten this problem out.

Supervisor: Really? I never thought of that.

You: I'll be in your area on a consulting assignment later this week. Why don't I stop by to see you at 9:00 on Thursday morning?

Supervisor: I'm on a very limited budget. What do you charge?

You: Why don't we see whether I can be of assistance first. There won't be any charge at all. If I can do you some good, we can discuss it further. However, it appears we'll be able to reduce the costs substantially at Company X without a major change.

Supervisor: OK, you're on.

You: Thanks. I estimate we'll be about an hour.

Supervisor: Fine.

You: I'm looking forward to meeting you! See you then.

Supervisor: Sounds good. Bye.

You: Goodbye.

While the call can start differently and take an infinite number of turns, you are controlling the dialogue. It should *be* a dialogue, *not* two monologues. Listen actively, but don't give away your valuable advice when clients are willing to pay for it. How much is too much? Anything beyond "just enough." You're giving away the sample, not selling the product.

Abraham Lincoln said it, and every lawyer knows it:

Your time and advice are your stock in trade.

Fee or free, which will it be?

You may have to leave a few messages before you swing into action. If the supervisor calls back, *always* be courteous but too busy to talk. Ask if you can return the call in a "few minutes." This makes you appear in demand. It then enables you to organize your thoughts, review your notes, drink a cup of coffee (please), and relax. Then by initiating the call, your control position is increased.

In studying the consultant phone call, you'll note that the emphasis is on helping someone else. We are utilizing one of the most basic success principles ever discovered:

You will get what you want, if you give others what they want.

The call also considers the natural insecurity of anyone who depends upon another for emotional and financial support. It is a success principle etched in bronze on a plaque in our office:

There's a big difference between advising and assisting.

The call utilizes another success principle that makes it so dramatically effective:

Don't mention you are looking for a job.[14]

As you finesse around the gatekeeper, be completely honest. Subterfuge and misrepresentation destroy your self-respect, and you'll blow your cover. Your credibility will be damaged, and if you do get a consulting interview, it won't be a consoling one.

Avoid making consultant appointments after lunch. By the afternoon, the supervisor is probably running behind on projects started in the morning, sluggish from lunch, preoccupied, and disoriented. Call in the morning, about one hour after start of business, when your prospect is receptive. This gives you time to arrive early and scope out the situation, too.

As you start arranging appointments, you'll penetrate that "hidden job market." You'll know it's only "hidden" *because* it's so obvious—it's *everywhere! You* were hiding by not seeking!

26. Telephone timing is everything (almost).

Good timing measurably increases the number of interviews. There are times your call will connect and times it "disconnects." Statistically, the best time to reach an interviewer in the personnel department is any Tuesday through Friday between 9:00 A.M. and 11:00 A.M.

Mondays are unpredictable and should be avoided. There's probably a deluge of calls from weekend ads, Friday's backlog, and new hires to process. As I mentioned in *Jeff Allen's Best: The Resume*, your paperwork will get lost in the shuffle on Monday. Your telephone call (if taken) will be heard with the wrong ear— the one connected to the side of the brain that rejects applicants.

Friday mornings are particularly opportune since employees are terminating and hiring decisions are not made on Fridays. This means the interviewer may learn for the first time that a requisition exists and will defer discussing the position with you by arranging an interview.

Friday afternoons are even worse than Monday mornings since "exit interviews" are being conducted. These are the "back end" of a personnel position. The farther away you are, the better.

Mornings from Tuesday through Friday are also good times to reach departmental decision makers and the "getwork network" that will assist you in setting up interviews. Use that fertile phone time wisely.

Weave Your "Getwork Network"

The first and most important use of the phone is to learn what your contacts know about job opportunities and obtain their assistance.

W-w-w-what did you say? Hold the phone! Don't worry—I'm going to put you in touch with powerful contacts you didn't even *know* you had!

Chapter

3

Network—All the
Way to Work

"Networking" became a buzzword in the 1970s, but it's been around a lot longer than that. When you set out to get your first job, you probably heard your "elders" say, "It's not *what* you know, it's *who* you know." Then, it was known as being "well connected." Nothing's changed except the word and the number of books written on the subject.

Actually, "networking" really says it all: it's a *net* to keep you *working*. You cast it in a variety of ways, which I'll discuss in this chapter.

In the late 1970s, career authors jumped on the "networking" bandwagon. Job hopefuls were told to call contacts and make "network" appointments rather than interview appointments under the guise of asking for advice or "conducting a survey." They were supposed to leave each appointment with at least two other names.

Formal and informal "career networks" sprang up. Some people made careers out of networking! One even claimed he could get in touch with *anyone* with a maximum of three phone calls.

Pretty soon, networking was getting in the way of working, and people went back to "getworking" again. Networking didn't stop, though. It just became what it had been before: the secret success weapon in every superstar's arsenal.

As Kenneth and Sheryl Dawson noted in *Job Search: The Total System*:

> We're well aware that networking has fallen into disfavor among "savvy" job hunters. Many self-anointed "experts" now claim that networking is passe, that the American job market has been just about networked to death. Well, we

dismiss that nonsense out of hand. Successful job hunters are like salmon swimming upstream. The one percent courageous enough to go against the current instinctively struggle to reach the river's source. Although the majority of job searchers looking for an easy placement float downstream, the *one percenters* who take control of their campaigns know that they must go against the current to get to where the jobs are.

This is not meant to minimize the difficulties of networking. The reason this concept has slipped from its favored status among job search "experts" who are always looking for a hot fad is simply because too many people use it unprofessionally. Each time some jerk calls a company executive without a conversational agenda, without direction, and without goals, he wastes everyone's time. As a consequence, the road is that much rougher for everyone who follows. Your task will be that much more challenging.

Just because networking is misused, abused, and trivialized by amateurs doesn't mean that you must choose an alternative. Quite simply, there are none. U.S. Department of Labor Statistics prove that 80 percent of people who find jobs in this country do so by networking. . . .Effective networking gets jobs. The more you do it and the better you do it, the sooner you'll be selecting the best positions from among several offers.[15]

The techniques that follow offer ways for you to cultivate your own getwork network of colleagues, acquaintances, and friends—and activate it to get interviews.

27.   Mine the gold of personal contacts.

Make a *comprehensive* list of everyone you know. Don't be too selective—you're not inviting them over for a job club meeting, only writing down their name and number. Then cast your net to find out what they know about companies that are hiring and jobs you'd like to do. You'll be surprised what information is available for the asking. Work that personal network. As I noted in *Finding the Right Job at Midlife,* there are two ways personal contacts should be used:

> *Notifying you about opportunities.* Their motivation to assist is best utilized by asking them to be your eyes and ears. Helping you enhances their own self-esteem. They often delight in letting you know inside information or leads that they learned about through personal observation. You should *gently* let them know if they are furnishing information on jobs that you don't want. Be grateful for any assistance, no matter how ridiculous, or you may lose more than a resource and a reference—you may lose someone who really cares . . .

> *Presenting your background.* Since they are your acquaintances, they will be working for you with the best intentions. Therefore, copies of your . . . resume and other background information should be given to them. Retype the resume, deleting anything you feel is too personal but giving them as much data as you can.

> While personal contacts are a limited resource, they are only limited by your willingness to "cold call." . . . [A] complete stranger can become a friend on the telephone in a matter of minutes. . . .

> The cold call of today is often the reference of tomorrow, so you should look at the relationship as strictly business, intending to reciprocate. Until you're situated, try to finesse around personal meetings with new acquaintances, unless there's really a job opening. They can neutralize the powerful telephone advantage and waste too much . . . time.

> *Everybody* is a "closet applicant" for the right job, so there is a natural identification with someone seeking employment. A short note with [your] resume enclosed will restate your contact information, background, and appreciation.[16]

28. Profit from professional contacts.

Your accountant, lawyer, stockbroker, insurance agent, financial planner—anyone whose services you've purchased—can be a great resource. One of their clients or professional contacts could easily be your next employer.

The following procedure is much like that outlined in Tip 27. A telephone call, followed by information in the mail, ended with results. It should go something like this:

Receptionist: Good morning, Brophy & Associates, Certified Public Accountants.

Mark: Good morning, I'd like to speak to Dean Brophy, please. This is Mark Gibson calling.

Receptionist: One moment, Mr. Gibson.

Dean: Mark! Good morning. I didn't expect to hear from you until tax season—is there something I can do for you?

Mark: As a matter of fact, Dean, there is. You know when we got together earlier this year I told you I went back to school to complete my M.B.A? My job as an engineer had stalled, and I saw the M.B.A. as an effective way to give my career a boost.

Dean: I remember. How's it going?

Mark: Well, it's been a long haul, but I'm almost ready to graduate and I'm organizing my job search. When we talked, you mentioned that a client—a small steel company—was in need of reorganization. Do you think they could use a structural engineer with an M.B.A. from a good school to help streamline them? My concentration is in finance, and I have a lot of steel experience.

Dean: I'm glad you called. We're just about to pull together a new management team. I'd forgotten our last conversation, but your qualifications might be just what we need. How about if you and I get together and talk this week, and then we'll arrange to meet with the client. Can you be here Thursday at 4:00?

Mark: I'll be there. I'll stop by today and drop off my resume for you to review in the meantime.

Dean: Great. I'm looking forward to it, Mark. There's a lot of potential at this company, but it needs direction to get where it belongs.

Mark: I already have some ideas. Let's discuss them Thursday and take it from there. I'll see you then.

Dean: Good enough. Bye.

Mark: Goodbye.

That dialogue was representative of the actual experience of one jobseeker who went from an anonymous midlevel job in a large company to a successful top management one at a smaller company—all because he picked up the phone.

The job wasn't advertised—85 percent of all jobs aren't. No job you ever got was, right? Of *course* I'm right. People don't get hired from ads. Ads are usually placed to give the *appearance* of hiring or to test the market. By the time they hit the paper, the *average* time from internally identifying an opening to placing an ad is around six months. So, chasing after that 15 percent will get you tired long before you're hired. Even worse, it will make you wonder what's wrong with you. That's the only "truth in advertising" you need to know.

29. Rent a mentor.

A mentor is a combination father, mother, teacher, public relations person, coach, bodyguard, and guide. No doubt you've already heard how important it is in business to have a mentor—an elder tribesperson who will protect and guide you through the corporate jungle. Someone who has your best interests at heart, and wants to see you get a better job. However, as I wrote in *Surviving Corporate Downsizing*:

> With qualifications like that, you can bet there are many more "mentees" than mentors to ment them. It would be great if you could just pick out some senior citizen at work and ment away. But you can't. Even if you could find one, it takes time and ongoing communication to develop a lasting friendship. You'll just have to rent a mentor.

> Your boss is your most likely choice....The reason your boss is a rent-a-mentor is that he's probably not going to risk jeopardizing his position to help you. He's also probably not one of the major movers in the company.[17]

You didn't need your boss to help you there, though. He or she is more effective in helping you get hired somewhere else. His or her reference *alone* is a jobseeking jewel.

Once you discover how valuable a strong mentor relationship can be, you'll never look for a job without one again. Become a "mentee." "Rent" a mentor who will take you to the top.

30. Sport a sponsor.

A sponsor is a mentor magnified to the power of 10. This person not only coaches and protects you, but manages you, too. A sponsor helps you be seen and heard—where it counts.

A sponsor usually *is* one of the prime movers in the company. Through diligence and proper self-promotion, you can find someone to sponsor you. Most sponsors won't waste their time with people who can't perform, so be sure you're ready for sponsorship before you ask.

Your positive performance after you're hired helps your sponsor look good.

Beware of pseudosponsors. They're the deceptive delegators who take credit for someone else's effort. Your name and face will never enter a corporate boardroom if you help the wrong person look good. That's the deal—you help in exchange for sponsorship.

31. Infiltrate the secretarial secret service.

The secretarial secret service can make or break you. To get interviewed, infiltration is important. As I noted in *Surviving Corporate Downsizing*:

> Even in the smallest companies, the secretaries generally call

the shots. . . . [T]heir responsibilities, knowledge, influence with their bosses, and constant communication with each other make them extremely powerful. Collectively, they form an organization within an organization—the secretarial "secret service." Its chart looks like a grapevine.

If you are in management, infiltration into the secretarial ranks must be vicarious. It starts with a recognition of the importance of the one who is performing *your* clerical duties (clerk typist, stenographer, secretary, assistant, etc.). If you have ever lost this capability when you needed to send a letter, find a missing file, answer a phone, run an errand, or just talk, you require no further convincing. Mutual respect and loyalty are imperative.

Secretaries are continuously exposed to the latest rumors and gossip, which gives them the opportunity to detect changes long before they occur. The sources of the information are other secretaries who prepare the correspondence, organization charts, personnel status changes, job requisitions, termination notices, final checks, and the myriad other documents that affect your job.

For this reason, you should mentally deputize your secretary as your official secret agent. Let her take her coffee breaks, do her photocopying, deliver the documents, and attend the social functions. Listen carefully to her observations. She's your partner, your ally, your confidante, your "eyes and ears," your image-maker, and your alter ego. Oh yes, she's also your clerk.

Don't forget her birthday; Valentine's Day (February 14), even if you are the same sex; Secretary's Day (the third Wednesday in April), although she insists she's not a secretary; Secretary's Week (the third week in April); and holidays. Any time she works extra hard, give her time off; take her to a business lunch; buy her flowers, candy, or show tickets (two, but you're not invited); or just write her a thank-you note. Fight to give her a raise. Understand if she's trying to manage a family. It's so important and so easily overlooked. Do it at the first opportunity.

Mark your calendar with these "secretarial" dates and set up accounts with local florists and candy shops that accept phone orders and deliver. Buy a supply of quality thank you-notes and keep them in your desk. You want the reward to be as close to the effort as possible. A little genuine, well-timed appreciation goes a long way.

Respect should be accorded other secretaries as well. Depending on the manager, a secretary may actually run the department. Even if you suspect she is making decisions in her boss's name, accept them as you would from him.[18]

Good relations with those who control the flow of information are essential. These contacts continue to serve you even after you've moved on.

32. Invite yourself to join the in-crowd.

"Company insiders" know what's going to happen before it does. Those who have the inside track benefit from money crunches, reorganizations, and downsizes. In-crowd membership has its privileges.

In high school you probably called them "cliques." If you shunned them there, you probably do at work. But if you're in a large organization, there are only three positions to choose from: in, out, or in the middle. If you can stay in the middle without alienating one or more factions, you're extraordinary. If you try to succeed alone, you'll depressingly discover—as every politician does—that you can't succeed without support.

And, as I noted with reference to corporate power bases in *Surviving Corporate Downsizing*:

> [T]he only difference between a Republican and a Democrat is that one is in office, and the other isn't. This is also true in the corporate world, but there are usually no outward signs of "who's who in the zoo."

Infiltrating into the right "in-group" or "clique" requires taking a few steps back and asking yourself (and perhaps some trusted coworkers) where the factions are. If you've been working for a while and don't know, it's only because they're below the surface. You've got to find them right away, so here are five signs to watch.

When certain employees:

1. Constantly meet with the boss and others above him.
2. Receive a better office, preferential work, seminar approvals, reimbursement, and more smiles from supervisors.
3. Have similar ages, religions, political views, opinions, speech patterns, vocabularies, eating and drinking habits, and ways of dressing.
4. Cluster together at breaks and other times they are off duty.
5. Are promoted or get raises faster for no apparent reason.

There are others, but these are enough to define the cliques. *Infiltration* is just a matter of *imitation*. You don't have to change your entire belief system. No job is worth that. There's a strategic reason for not doing so as well: "In-groups" can become "out-groups" overnight. They are held together only by friendship and loyalty—not very strong bonds in the "what-have-you-done-for-me-lately" business world. . . .

[A]lign yourself with *several* cliques, even if they oppose each other, breaking through their stares and actively listening to the members, and agreeing where you can. This is referred to as "enlightened fence sitting" by conflict analysts, but it's more like fence *jumping*. Strange as it sounds, an open mind is often the entry into a clique. But you must make the first move. Start by saying, "Do you mind if I join you for lunch? I'd like to get to know you and your friends better."

Although inappropriate with your boss, you can (and should) use the lunch hour for developing a bond with coworkers. United you sit; divided you fall—down.

You should go out to lunch twice a week with influential members of a clique. This is an important program to begin, because you will start having common outside experiences (which cannot be done on breaks). A coalition develops, and you'll be picking up a lot of information that can be valuable to you or your boss.[19]

If you thought "working hard" was all that was necessary for success, I hope this advice prompts you to think again. Any time more than two people are together, power enters the room.

Being aware of the balance of power—and managing it to your advantage—will give you information about openings in other companies. When a member of your in-crowd moves to another company, keep in touch. You never know. . . .

---

33. Align with the company-liners.

A variation of an in-crowd are groups of employees known as company-liners. They may be found huddled together, or throughout the organization. They're recognized by their yesses to higher-ups and yuks at their jokes. They wear service pins and display company awards in their offices.

Company-liners often become senior executives because they internalize company goals, communicate them to their staffs, and "execute" corporate policies. In *Surviving Corporate Downsizing* I noted:

> Infiltration into the "company-liner" ranks is relatively simple and extremely safe. It is generally done by:
>
> 1. Openly stressing the importance of "doing a good job" and using company slogans, if they exist.
> 2. Extolling the virtues of the company.
> 3. Suggesting ways to improve operations wherever possible (reducing costs, increasing efficiency, developing new products, etc.).
> 4. Never, *never* publicly criticizing anything about the management or direction of the company.[20]

Following these four simple rules will increase your likelihood of long-term employment, with regular promotions, with your current employer. It can help you with job references when you set out for greener pastures, as well.

34. Associate in associations.

Professional association meetings make the site a candy store for contacts. That's why almost everyone is there, and members network aggressively. Some groups even call themselves "career networks."

Whether you join an association in your specialty or a non-trade association, don't sit silently through the program and leave. Network like a native nut. Volunteer for committees that will increase your visibility and your proximity. Run for office. Leverage yourself outside the restricted radius of your job.

Scan trade journals and your local paper for notices of meetings. Visit the library and look up your specialty in *The Encyclopedia of Associations*. Check out membership fees, ask for contact information about members in your area, and talk to them. Get their opinions of the value of the organization. Form your opinion of them. Attend a few meetings without making a membership commitment. The first one can be misleading, since members are on their best behavior.

35. On the road, be kind to the people you find.

Remember the person who sat next to you on that flight and talked when you had work to do?

Don't confuse this motormouth with the tactful talker who finds common interests, asks interesting questions, and *listens* to the answers. Some of the best business relationships on the ground began in midair on a plane. Even more began at an airport waiting gate, the van to a hotel, and inside its lobby. When two business travelers exchange business cards, global networking occurs. It never stops, either. In fact, it's what makes the working world go 'round.

36. Continue friendships with coworkers and supervisors.

If you have been working at weaving, your network includes former coworkers and supervisors. You just have to start smiling and dialing.

But, if you're the type who crosses bridges without ever looking back, you'll need to retrace your steps. You may even have to reintroduce yourself. The potential for interview contacts aside, former colleagues and supervisors can be valuable references (more in Chapter 4)—which is another source of interviews.

Begin by making a list of everyone you know from working. Then call and find out if they're still there, if they remember you, and if they have any ideas about potential career opportunities.

37. Cultivate current business contacts outside your employer.

This includes customers, vendors, and consultants to your current employer. Those who rely on your company's business may not want to talk as readily. But developing a relationship with key people in these companies can provide valuable insights and job leads. They'll answer if asked properly. Include key people from these three sources on your getwork network.

38. Access academic allies.

Former professors, deans, administrators, advisors, and classmates all shared an important part of your life. You can retrace your academic life to develop contacts for your search. This is particularly valuable if you attended graduate school. Many professors of law, business, medical, and engineering schools are working in the field.

Alumni association activities and newsletters are other great ways to communicate with your academic allies. Perhaps your college placement office even offers career networking. Most schools provide ongoing placement assistance—formally or informally—to graduates. Call yours and you may find those tuition payments now pay back career dividends.

39. Obtain information from editors and writers for trade journals.

Their names are listed on the "masthead" (at the beginning of most publications, the back of others). They probably have the names and numbers of most of the movers and shakers in your business in their files. Writers and editors network most of the day, so they readily share information. They realize that helping you might result in another story. Besides, fostering alumnus uninterruptus is their job.

If you call and get through to them when they're on a deadline, don't expect much. Call back in a week. They'll be staring at a blank screen, sputtering to get started on the next issue, and might update your life as the first piece.

40. Attend meetings of chambers of commerce and civic groups.

Interview leads may be as close as your own backyard—or the main street of your home town. You don't have to own a business to attend chamber of commerce "mixers" and mix like a mixmaster.

Similarly, you can become involved in Rotary, Jaycees, and other groups that networked mercilessly long before the word was used.

Consider the caution in Tip 34, however. When joining any group, maintain your perspective. You join just for job leads, but you don't want to waste career prime time, either. Be active in the organization (because if you don't give, you won't get), but don't be hyperactive. Voluntary associations will take as much as you can give—and ask for more. It's up to you to draw the line. Besides, you'll have more time to volunteer once you're settled in your new job. Right now, your most important cause is *vocational* volunteering. Nothing more.

41. Join job networks.

There are a variety of national, regional, local, and specialized job networks around. Most have meetings, resume exchanges, and newsletters listing job openings.

Some are full-scale, profit-driven operations. Others are informal, voluntary, job-sharing clubs. All are worth considering. The value of the leads varies so widely that generalization is impossible. One generalization is accurate, though—none will get you hired.

Look in the job market publications I discuss in Chapter 6 for the names of networks. Call and ask about their service, procedure, and fees. Then request a copy of their brochure, application, and most recent newsletter. It will help you decide whether there's any point in joining.

42. Follow the five-step networking process.

In *Job Search*, the Dawsons suggested five steps for effective networking:

- *Step 1: Prepare your contact list.* Include not just important decision-makers but everyone who may be able to help you. Also include your list of target companies.
- *Step 2: Send a resume and cover letter to each of your primary contacts.* Just because a contact happens to be your brother, you're making an egregious mistake if you assume he knows all there is to know about you and your career. . . .

  [More on cover letters in Chapter 5.]

- *Step 3: Use your contacts properly.* Be aware that your network will usually think more in terms of jobs open or not open than in terms of your individual skills and background. Help keep each contact focused on you—on what you've done before and can do in the future as well as on how potential employers might use your skills and experience. Remember to offer your assistance to your contacts in any way possible.

- *Step 4: Always ask permission to use the name of your contact.* Then do just that, both in phone conversations and in correspondence. Nothing drives the networking process more quickly and more effectively than a personal reference. That's how you break through into secondary and tertiary contacts. Always open the conversation or letter with a phrase such as "A mutual acquaintance, John Robertson, suggested that I contact you." The body of the letter (or phone conversation) should very briefly summarize who you are and why you're making contact. Then close with a proactive statement about calling or visiting soon to discuss mutually beneficial plans.

- *Step 5: Follow up.* Again, let your contact set the schedule. Just be certain that you adhere to it and recontact each person within the agreed-upon time. Report back to your contact when a lead pans out. It's not only professional to do this, but it keeps that person aware of and interested in what you're doing and where you're going. Even if a secondary contact doesn't develop into a job lead, when you keep your primary contacts advised, you're inevitably drawing them closer to your corner for future contacts and assistance. This is how psychological leverage works in networking. In your initial contact, you've offered to help them in any way possible. You've been thorough, courteous, and professional in following up each time, and now you're reporting back with a progress update and another thank-you.

Always keep your goals foremost in your mind for each contact. First, you want leads about openings. Failing that, you want the names of other people in the firm or elsewhere with whom you might talk. Keep pushing, deepening, and broadening your network.[21]

43. Maintain your network.

Once you get tuned into networking—and it works for you—
don't stop. Establishing a network takes time and diligence.
Maintaining it takes more. It's an ongoing give-to-get process.
But the rewards appear when you press the right combination of
buttons on your phone and instant job leads answer.

Next Step: Secure a Super-reference

Now, let's go on to Chapter 4, where your network groupies
become job references to get you interviews.

Chapter

4

References: Position Power to Propel You to the Top

I wrote *The Perfect Job Reference* for all serious searchers. It gave a step-by-step, detailed explanation of the whys and hows of references. As I noted:

> The powerful third-party role of a reference can be either terrific or terrible, depending on you. Your reference check doesn't have to be a *test* (that you take blindly, wondering if you'll "pass"); it can be a *testimonial*. A properly constructed reference letter can get you an interview, and a properly instructed reference can get you hired.[22]

The key to turning a benign "to-whom-it-may-concern" reference into a potent *super-reference* is *positioning*. The position of your reference, the way you are positioned by your reference in a letter or telephone call, targeting a specific position, and someone in a position to hire for it are all essential elements of a super-reference.

The following techniques are summarized from *The Perfect Job Reference*.

44. Pick perfect professional references.

By only considering former supervisors or college instructors as references, most jobseekers neglect 80 percent of the potential reference population.

Supervisors are an important source of references to be sure. Most employers want to know what people who ordered you around thought of your obedience. But there's more to know about you. Besides, employers understand if you don't want your current supervisor contacted until you've accepted their offer.

The previous section on networking suggested the sources of reference power you can tap to supercharge your search.

It's more secure to begin your search without current supervisors knowing, too. Successful seekers want to keep their search secret. Current employers just don't understand career desire.They call it unkind things like "heresy," "treason," and "involuntary termination." (The rent-a-mentor boss mentioned in Tip 29 is a notable exception.)

Review your career history and your current business contacts for the names of influential references who can give you search security without job jeopardy. Your list might include:

- Former supervisors.
- Your boss's boss and other high-level executives at past employers who knew your contributions.
- Coworkers at present or past employers who witnessed your skills and effectiveness.
- Subordinates who can verify your management ability.
- Colleagues or others who served with you on committees or task forces.
- Members of trade associations or other professional groups who know you.
- Managers of support departments who assisted with your projects. These include managers of Human Resources, Finance, Management Information Systems, Communications, Sales, Marketing, Market Research, Purchasing, Inventory Control, and so on.
- Key employees of consulting firms and other vendors whose services were contracted by your employer and who worked with you directly. Consultants often have contacts—and clout—nationwide.
- Key employees of client and supplier firms.

Be careful with the last two types. These potentials might want to help, but their own company policies prevent them from doing so. Don't pressure them—you could destroy future references if they change jobs.

Once you've created your list, start smiling and dialing, using these guidelines from *The Perfect Job Reference*:

Lock up at least *six* references suitable for framing—those who are glad to hear from you, and whose wondrous words will improve your chances of getting that target job. If you don't have at least a half-dozen, half-crazed, wide-eyed professional references to take with you into an interview, call *more*.

Cross off people who greet you with, "Joe Who?" and who never seem to understand that you're not from the unemployment office. Cut the call short when the prospective reference speaks unintelligibly or calls you something unkind. Search until you find the motivated maniacs who will be glad to help you. Be sure there are no hidden agendas (such as reference revenge on jolly jobseekers).

Your references must mention the attributes and skills that will get you hired. The owner of the garage where you worked during college might be able to comment on your ability to adjust a carburetor. But, if you're supposed to be an expert in process control, that reference needs a tune-up! Help him to remember your promptness, mechanical genius, and ability to complete your work properly. If you don't put the rabbits in his hat, don't expect him to pull them out. All the words in the world won't replace the few magic ones you tell him.

Just by living, every person develops a cadre of references—known and unknown, good and bad. We're just ensuring they'll be *known*, then *good*. Let's say one job requires an ability to supervise. You trot out all the references who can attest to your management skills. Another job might require analytical skills. Revive the staff accountant from your last job. Resuscitate a statistics professor who taught a graduate course you took. Think ahead, so your reference roll reflects everyone that will be important when the roll is called.[23]

45. Pick perfect personal references.

Placement professionals have their own definition of the term "personal reference": those who depend on jobseekers for support or who owe them money. For years, the names that were dutifully listed on an application form under "Personal References" were people no self-respecting employer would consider.

But times have changed. With all the constraints (legal and otherwise) now limiting what companies can and will say about a former employee, personal references are a potent source for getting interviews. In fact, they're becoming *preference references*—the winner's edge in the placement race.

The *right* list of personal references is the key to success in securing interviews. Each should:

- Consent to give a reference about you.
- Have a surname different from yours (even if related).
- Work in an office where he or she can receive calls during business hours, and can privately tell (rhymes with "sell") about you intelligently, credibly, and enthusiastically.
- Be thoroughly prepared by you to give a knowledgeable, motivational, inspirational reference.

As you create your list of preference references (at least 50 candidates from which you should select 5), look for these additional attributes:

- A successful professional life.
- A self-confident, upbeat, outgoing demeanor.
- Good oral and written communication skills.
- A fondness for you (with a little PR, if necessary).
- A desire (preferably burning) to help you succeed.

46.   Prime your perfect references properly.

If you've worked your getwork network of professional and personal contacts, activating it now to secure super-references involves three simple steps:

*   *Step 1: The initial telephone call.* After a brief greeting and exchange of pleasantries, move right to the purpose of your call. Here's an example from from *The Perfect Job Reference*:

    Joe, good to hear your voice again! It's Sam Stone. Did you get that article I sent last month on semiconductor research?

    (Friendly greeting, grateful acknowledgment)

    My pleasure. I wasn't sure if you subscribed to that journal, and I thought the article might relate to your area.

    But, I have another reason for calling. I'll only keep you a minute. I've decided it's time to move on. The reorganization here has limited the opportunity for advancement, so I've decided to look around for a director position. This is confidential, of course.

    Since we've worked closely together in the past, I'd be honored if you'd provide a professional reference. Your great reputation in the industry would help to verify my credentials. Will you assist me?[24]

Here is another example of an initial telephone call to a perfect personal reference:

Howard, this is Betty Brown.

Hi, Betty! I've been meaning to call and ask you what you're using on your roses this year. They look great.

Why, thank you! I'll have to refer that question to the family gardener. Frank takes care of the yard.

I'd really like to know. I haven't had any luck with mine. What can I do for you?

Well, I just passed the CPA exam, and I want to make a career move now. Foster Plastics is a great company, and it was convenient to work in town while the kids were young. But now I'm ready for a larger organization. I thought I'd target the insurance industry.

Sounds good. Congratulations on your certification. That was a lot of work. I wish I knew someone to recommend. I'm afraid I can't be much help.

Howard, you can be a *big* help. I'd like to use your name as a personal reference. We worked closely together on last year's school budget campaign, and I was impressed by your energy, your effectiveness, and your ability to communicate. I hoped your observations of me were equally good, and that you wouldn't mind saying so in a letter.

I'm honored to be asked! I couldn't have done all I did without your assistance in supplying the numbers to support our arguments. Talk about analytical skill! The Board of Ed is still talking about the accuracy of your projections.

If you'd put those thoughts into a short letter for me, I'd be most appreciative. With your power of expression, I can't lose.[25]

With such optimistic openers, you're bound to get only "Yes" for an answer. When you do, briefly mention the objective of your search and the company(ies) you're targeting. Then go on to Step 2.

- *Step 2: Send a copy of your resume and other pertinent information.* In addition to your resume, send your potential references a summary of the work you did together to refresh their memories, along with a list of questions they might be asked during a telephone reference check. (See Tip 49 for a list of questions for professional references, and Tip 50 for a list of questions for personal references.) This should be mentioned in a concise cover letter that closes by stating you will call to follow up.

- *Step 3: Follow up.* Call each reference back within a week after sending your materials to discuss the form and content of the letter they will write (Tips 47 and 48) as well as what to expect from reference telephone calls (Tips 49 and 50). If you haven't already supplied them with the addresses of target companies (including the names of decision makers), do it now.

Follow through to make sure you get the letter in a specified time, and then communicate throughout your search to let them know how it's going. During the process, many of your references will probably provide additional leads.

47. Create the perfect professional reference telephone call.

Most of the time, professional reference calls are *anything* but professional. Most people who are called to give a professional reference are caught off guard. They haven't been notified, or if they have, they haven't been properly prepared. Furthermore, they don't usually recall the highlights of the subject's career at their company. (Sorry—you're not an exception to the rule.)

If you follow the techniques in this section, *your* professional telephone references will be different. Whether they're called to verify your resume before scheduling an interview or after it, your references will be professional all right—professional announcers who will advertise you.

Your initial telephone calls served as an "audition" for the best ones. After selecting the best, meet with them (or talk thoroughly over the phone), give them their scripts, and rehearse them to deliver their winning performance about yours.

You need four things to give (or send) to each of your references:

- A sample completed application. (Applications are available from employers by calling and asking for them to be mailed. Stationery stores also have ones you can buy.)
- Your resume. (Only a *super-resume* will do. See the first book in this series, *Jeff Allen's Best: The Resume*, if you don't have one.)
- Your individualized "reference summary" (an example follows).
- The Professional Reference Questions list.

The last two items on the list were detailed in *The Perfect Job Reference*:

The Reference Summary

Most professional references are less interested in reading resumes than overworked personnel staffers. They want sales training, not reading lessons. That means "sizzle"— "closers" in the form of inspirational, motivational, believable experiences with you.

Your homework includes a brief, neatly typed, one-page summary (preferably with short headings) that reviews the significant facts in your references' eyewitness testimony. Concentrate on traits, skills, and accomplishments that apply to target jobs.

See, for example, the following sample reference summary.

Name: *John R. Smith*
Tel No.: (917) 321-8732

Former Title: *National Sales Manager*

ACCOMPLISHMENTS
- Supervised and motivated a field sales force that grew from 12 people to 20 during three-year tenure. Managed and led in-house sales support staff of six.
- Set and monitored sales objectives by territory and prod-

uct, resulting in an average annual increase in sales of 30%, with an overall three-year cumulative increase of 120% (from $6 million in 1980 to $13.2 million in 1983).

- Purchased and installed computerized sales monitoring and reporting system.
- Used customer feedback to help create and market three new products, the Accu Soft, the Accu Sort, and the Accu Scan, which are consistently among the top sellers produced by the company.
- Established a sales incentive program that increased sales across the board, and more than 50 percent each in the two lowest performing territories.

TRAITS
- Fast-moving, effective, results-oriented.
- Highly skilled at motivating others to achieve their goals.
- Reliable, loyal, enthusiastic.

Be honest, but not modest. Modesty in references telegraphs uncertainty, concealment, and even misrepresentation. Few references will overstate beyond your data, but many will understate. So give them every syllable you want them to say. Do it right, and you might even get a call like this:

"Hey, John, I got this list you sent me. What's wrong with you? You didn't say anything about the increased system sales and the time you won the national sales award!"

Prepare a summary for each reference, and keep a copy for *your* reference during your interviews.

The Professional Reference Questions List

The third item you will give each reference is two versions of a list of questions they are likely to be asked in a telephone reference check. The first will have "suggested" answers completed by you. This helps them "remember." (Your secret's safe with me.) Perhaps they never knew you when you worked together or what you did. No matter. What's wrong with a little help to help helpers help? They're not on trial—you are. And they're not under oath. Act too technical about this, and you might as well call some stranger and say, "I couldn't stand working with you and wouldn't ask you for a reference anyway."

Give each of your references a copy of the blank list, so they can use the completed one and other data to answer it in their own words. They won't, but it shows respect.

Professional Reference Questions

How long have you known _____?

How do you know _____ ?

When was he/she hired? _____

When did he/she leave? _____

What was his/her salary when he/she left? _____

Why did he/she leave? _____

Did you work with him/her directly? _____

Was he/she usually on time? _____

Was he/she absent from work very often?_____

Did his/her personal life ever interfere with his/her work?

_____

What were his/her titles? _____

What were his/her duties? _____

Did he/she cooperate with supervisors? _____

Did he/she cooperate with coworkers? _____

Did he/she take work home very often? _____

What are his/her primary attributes? _____

_____

What are his/her primary liabilities? _____

Is he/she eligible for rehire? _____

Can you confirm the information he/she has given?

_____

Of course, review any sensitive areas. If you were going through a divorce when you worked with your reference, and he or she remembers that your personal life interfered with your work (whose doesn't?), don't leave his or her response to chance. Say something like:

"I know I was going through some rough times during that period. I wouldn't have made it without your support. How will you answer questions about my attendance and productivity?"

Need I tell you the answer? Confront a ghost and it vanishes. Fear it, and it haunts your hunt. People don't tell the truth, even if they want to. They tell their *perception* of the truth.

Overcoming Objections

If a reference plainly objects to something you wrote in your preparation materials, or has a different memory of the past, listen carefully and make changes. It's rare, but you might hear:

"I don't know about this computerized sales reporting system you say you installed. I know you were involved, but the controller was really responsible. Could we just say you *participated* in choosing and installing a system?

(Your gracious reply, with a smile:)

"Of course. Your way really is more accurate, but it still sounds good. That's fine."

Then review the process, summarize the key points, and tell your references you will notify them of who will be calling, when, and why.[26]

48. Create the perfect personal reference telephone call.

The steps to follow are very similar to the steps for a perfect personal telephone reference. Your personal references, however, will need only

- Your resume.
- The reference summary.
- The Personal Reference Questions list.

The Reference Summary

For personal references, the reference summary is a one-page summary, or list, describing attributes and activities that (1) the reference can authenticate and (2) are relevant to your target job.

Here's the reference summary Betty Brown (Tip 46) gave Howard, her personal reference:

Sample Reference Summary

Name: *Betty R. Brown*
Telephone No. *(616) 522-3359*

Position Desired: *Accountant, Insurance Company*

CHARACTER TRAITS
- Determination
- Accuracy
- Thoroughness
- Commitment
- Follow-through
- Energy
- Enthusiasm
- Competence
- Positive attitude

JOB-RELATED ABILITIES AND SKILLS
- Compiled financial data and developed complete, accurate forecasts.
- Presented concise, understandable financial reports for budget projections.
- Demonstrated knowledge of accounting principles and procedures.

Prepare a similar summary to review with your references. This is the "wish-fulfillment list" that matches the prospective employer's wish list for the position you want. Be sure the references understand and agree with the contents.

Don't be embarrassed about selling yourself too much. You can't—your references need as much coaching as possible. Most will be grateful to be liberated from the task of describing you. They will be glad to have the adjectives and verbs on the summary when the reference checker calls.

As you review the individualized summary with each reference, be sure he or she understands:

- The objectives of your job search.
- The specific knowledge that you'd like him or her to relate in a reference call.
- The delivery necessary for maximum impact on the reference checker.

The summary may vary slightly if you are targeting more than one type of job. In that case, you may give each reference two or more summaries, each titled appropriately.

It is desirable for each list to be slightly different from the others. If you coach your references too well, and they are all using identical language, their recommendations will appear canned. The impact of spontaneity, candor, and credibility is lost.

The Personal Reference Questions List

The final item to give each reference is a duplicate list of questions they are likely to be asked by a reference checker. The first copy should have "suggested" answers written by you.

This is designed to be helpful, to refresh your reference's memory about dates and details of your relationship, and to make sure that what *you* say is verified by what your *references* say. It is the final step in the subtle, careful coaching process that prepares your eyewitness references to testify accurately and consistently to the facts you presented.

The second copy of the list you provide should be blank, without answers, to allow your references to use the information you have given them and their own recall to create their versions of their visions.

Personal Reference Questions

How long have you known _____?

How do you know _____?

What is your opinion of _____?

Does (he/she) get along well with others?_____

Is (he/she) usually on time?_____

Is (he/she) absent from work very often? _____

Does (he/she) bring work home very often? _____

Does (he/she) like (his/her) job? _____

What are (his/her) primary attributes? _____

_____

What are (his/her) primary liabilities? _____

_____

Trouble-Shooting

What is said to the reference checker is too important to be left unsaid by you. Even well-meaning references can reply inappropriately when they're unprepared.

Look carefully at the list. It contains loaded questions: *Is (he/she) easy to get along with? What are (his/her) primary liabilities?* Your coaching should prepare your references to be ready with a highly developed reply.

The completed reference summary prepared your references to discuss your "attributes." You can help them handle the question about liabilities equally well. Here are some answers that can transform liabilities into assets:

"Well, the one liability that comes to mind is that (he/she) considers (himself/herself) last. (He's/She's) never too busy to help someone or volunteer for another position. (He's/She's) one of those people who proves the truth of the phrase, If you want it done, give it to a busy person. It's funny, though. (He/She) never seems to get ruffled about it all. (He's/She's) organized, efficient, and goal-oriented. It seems that the more (he/she) does, the happier (he/she) is."

"(His/her) liabilities? Oh, I guess you could say (he's/she's) a workaholic! (He's/She's) canceled our Saturday morning tennis game on several occasions because (he/she) wanted to work on (his/her) projects while the office was quiet. Completing (his/her) work has consistently been (his/her) top priority. (He's/She's) very dedicated."

Always end a discussion of a liability or weakness by turning it into an *attribute* or *strength*.

"Is (he/she) easy to get along with?" can be a loaded question. Someone can be too "easy" if he or she is unable to say "No." In this case, the answer would be:

"(He/She) is firm, but fair. I've never seen (him/her) arbitrary; instead, (he/she) sets reasonable rules and expects them to be upheld. I've always found (him/her) very likable and concerned about the welfare of others, but (he/she) is no pushover."

These are your friends, remember! Arrange for enough time to explain your objectives, and show your references how they can help you achieve them. Meet personally over a quiet lunch or dinner (your treat, of course), and let them know how important this is to you. Give them your carefully prepared information, and go over it in detail.

Resist the temptation to give in when a personal reference says:

"Hey, I don't need your resume or any of this paperwork. I'll just tell them a bunch of lies. Don't worry. You'll sound great!"

Explain that it is important to you to sound great with the *facts*, and only those closest to you know just how to express them.

Follow-Up

Ask your references to accept the telephone calls or return them immediately (offering to pay any toll charges), and to notify you of the details the moment they hang up. You need the feedback and you need it *fast*.

When it's all over, and you're sitting in that fancy new office, remember to call all those people who "knew you when" to let them know you "remember them *now*."[27]

---

49. Prepare the perfect reference letter.

The perfect reference letter is *not* the traditional "To whom it may concern" letter that gets recycled with every search. The right reference letter for today's supercharged search is a *super-reference* letter. It's *written* by the right person, *targeted* to the right person (a decision maker), and contains *marketable information* about your skills and abilities. It's a cover letter for your resume that opens doors, inviting you in for interviews.

What someone else says about you has 10 times the impact of what you say about yourself. It's even greater if the person saying it is someone whose name, title, or reputation is respected by the target. This reference can be either personal or professional. But select the very best from both lists for this crucial task. Nothing will result in more interviews.

The super-reference letter is a concise, communicative, one-page letter from a carefully selected reference. Each letter should be personalized to individuals who either have (1) the authority to hire you or (2) connections to those who do. Each letter should be a signed original.

Chapter 5 contains specific information about cover letter form and content, then includes sample letters. The cover letter should be interesting and upbeat while remaining businesslike. If the reference knows the target personally, the letter can be slightly less formal.

The language should be persuasive, even enthusiastic. Getting your references to do this right is a major move. Rather than trying to coach such busy, influential people or letting them write these crucial interview-getters, write them yourself! Most references will be glad to let you do it. Many will even provide you with letterhead so that you can type originals for their signature.

If the reference is personally known to the target, the opening and closing paragraphs should be in the writer's own words. But you can supply the language for the midsection (known as the "value paragraph") where your attributes are advertised.

Use your judgment. Just be sure to find the right reference to impress and convince the right target to see you. Chapter 5 provides a crash course on cover letters of all kinds.

50. Repair ragged references.

While we're discussing references, let's consider what to do if there are some skeletons rattling around in your career closet. Silencing them now is essential for your peace of mind and an organized search. As I wrote in *The Perfect Job Reference*:

> If you were fired, resigned under duress, or left in the heat of battle, it's time to roll out your reference regalia. It needs repair.
>
> Even if you don't voluntarily disclose your former supervisor's name, don't think he or she won't be called. Many companies check all past employers. If you know (or suspect) that someone is just waiting for a chance to dump a little reference rubble on your records, you have two alternatives:
>
> 1. Have someone call pretending to be an employer seeking a reference. Determine exactly what is being said about you. If it's not the best sales job possible, call back two days later and use the technique [Tip 46] we discussed earlier. Most lukewarm references are the result of un-identified, untrained, unmotivated folks who just need a call from you. If you don't give them a reason to help or

    guidance about how to do it, don't expect them to extend themselves.

2. Confront your accuser. Telephone him or her, and be firm and forthright. Make sure your conversation is liberally sprinkled with the following legalese: *interference with contractual relations, interference with prospective economic advantage, defamation of character, slander, libel, fraud, conspiracy, punitive damages, exemplary damages, attorney's fees, costs of suit, litigation,* and *jury trial.* Nice talk. It not only makes you feel great, but it works even greater.

It is not likely that you'll receive an apology, though. Instead, you'll receive denials and promises to sell well. . . .

Find someone else in the same company who will give a good reference, too. Confronted references sometimes appear to be *contrived* ones. They have a tendency to crawl through the phone. Savvy personnelers "dual check" when they're suspicious.[28]

---

51. Get a super-reference signed by your current employer (when management knows you're leaving).

If you've undertaken your job search with your current employer's blessings (or answering its prayers), the time to negotiate a favorable reference is *before you leave.* This works especially well if the employer wants you out. Since you're cooperating, the company is likely to give you a favorable reference. Management rarely refuses, because it's a way for them to reduce their guilt (or their fear that you'll change your mind).

    Then, type a letter (on company letterhead) that emphasizes the positive aspects of your tenure, and prepare it for the signature of the highest ranking, most upbeat, genuinely interested person you can find. People dread writing references letters but sign them willingly. Prepare multiple originals for signature.

You can fill in the target names and addresses later, when you have them.

Then tell the reference that he or she may be called. Leave a completed application, resume, and script. Smile and thank him or her. When they hear from you again, it will be to thank them again and give them your new office number.

Next Up: Cover Letters

Chapter 5 is next with more techniques about reference cover letters, and all other cover letters, that will shift your search into overdrive.

Chapter

5

Cover Letters Uncover Interviews

All effective cover letters are:

- Upbeat.
- Concise.
- Direct.

These balanced, believable "better letters" result in interview after interview. Even if writing isn't your strength, the techniques in this section will help you develop a proven approach to communicating and motivating with letters.

Three specific types of interview-getting cover letters are discussed in this section:

- The reference resume cover letter.
- Your resume cover letter.
- The broadcast letter.

All three "cover" your resume and uncover your potential. Each subsection on these three types of letters includes a sample to get you started on drafting your own. Do it right and the phone will ring with requests for interviews. But, first, let's review the rules for all good letters.

52. Get the "better letter" look.

In *The Perfect Cover Letter*, Richard Beatty told how to create the right "look" for your cover letter:

The physical layout and design of a cover letter is important to its effectiveness for several reasons.

First, good layout and design enhance appearance and serve to create a favorable impression on the part of the reader. A letter that is well-designed, properly spaced, and neat will create a positive image of you as an individual. It will suggest to prospective employers that you are logical, neat, and well-organized. Conversely, an improperly or poorly designed letter can convey just the opposite and thus leave a negative impression.

Second, a neat, concise, and well-organized format will substantially improve readability and thereby enhance communications and increase the probability that your cover letter will be read. Additionally, a good format will properly highlight the important aspects of your credentials, thus improving the chances of successfully marketing yourself to prospective employers.

Third, failure to employ an acceptable business letter format may suggest that you are ignorant of common business practices or, worse, that you simply don't care. Neither impression will help your cause and may, in fact, detract substantially from your self-marketing efforts and your overall job hunting plan.[29]

These principles apply equally to all effective cover letters. In fact, they are the same for all business correspondence. It is more than a "cover"—it's a package. It's a preview of what's inside. It gets the recipient ready to buy.

Read and remember these rules for cover letter style:

- Each letter should be an original, never photocopied, signed in black ink.
- No letter should be more than one page long.
- Type each letter on a self-correcting typewriter (or word processor) with a carbon ribbon using 12-pitch type with margins no wider than 10 and 70.

- Address each letter completely with no abbreviations, and include the middle initial and title of the recipient.
- Don't precede the decision maker's name with "Mr.," "Ms.," or "Mrs." However, do use the designation in the greeting of the letter. (Use "Mrs." only if you're *sure* the recipient does.)
- Use the proper spelling of all names and the correct company name. Call to check if you're not sure.
- Don't address a decision maker in the greeting by his or her first name.
- Eliminate errors or erasures. ("White-out" is out, too.)
- Use only high-quality (personal or professional) letter-head.

53. Limit the body of the letter to four paragraphs:

a. The *introductory paragraph*, where the writer introduces himself or herself and mentions briefly how he or she knows you.

b. The *value paragraph*, which describes the applicant's background and highlights his or her attributes that will benefit the target company. It's the longest paragraph, but not more than five or six sentences. It should be sincere and persuasive.

c. The *action paragraph*, which asks the reader to read the resume enclosed and contact the applicant for an interview (or wait patiently for him or her to call).

d. A *closing paragraph*, which expresses appreciation.

54. Develop a simple writing style.

There should be no compound sentences or long paragraphs. Key points in italic or bold face type are appropriate if limited to no more than a total of five.

55. Use a block letter format.

Its features are:

- Indented return address and date.
- Spaces between paragraphs.
- Double-indented complimentary closing.
- Triple-indented signature line.

The block format is shown on the next page.

Study the cover letter examples given in this section and follow their approach. Your secret's safe with me. Note that each sample is interesting and readable. There are short, crisp sentences and concise paragraphs. Each thought bridges logically to the next. In a word, the letters move! And they move jobseekers into jobs.

56. Practice makes perfect cover letters!

Draft a few trial letters, then read them aloud—to yourself and others. If they don't pass the read-aloud test for clarity and interest, rewrite them. Make them powerful enough to open doors you literally didn't know existed.

Block Letter Format

```
                    (return address)    XXXXXXXXXXXXXXX
                                        XXXXXXXXXXXXXXX

                            (date)      XXXXXXXXXXXXXX

XXXXXXXXXXXXXXXXXX (address)
XXXXXXXXXXXXXXXXXX
XXXXXXXXXXXXXXXXXX

Re: XXXXXXXXXXXXXXXXXXXXXXXXX

XXXXXXXXXXXXXXXXXX (salutation)

XXXXXXXXXXXXXXXXXXXXXXXXXXXXXXXXXXXXXXXXXXXXXXXXXXXXXXXXXXXXXXXXX
XXXXXXXXXXXXXXXXXXXXXXXXXXXXXXXXXXXXXXXXXXXXXXXXXXXXXXXXXXXXXXXXX
XXXXXXXXXXXXXXXXXXXXXXXXXXXXXXXXXXXXXXXXXXXXXXXXXXXXXXXXXXXXXXXXX
XXXXXXXXXXXXXXXXXXXXXXXXXXXXXXXXXXXXXXXXXXXXXXXXXXXXXXXXXXXXXXXXX

XXXXXXXXXXXXXXXXXXXXXXXXXXXXXXXXXXXXXXXXXXXXXXXXXXXXXXXXXXXXXXXXX
XXXXXXXXXXXXXXXXXXXXXXXXXXXXXXXXXXXXXXXXXXXXXXXXXXXXXXXXXXXXXXXXX
XXXXXXXXXXXXXXXXXXXXXXXXXXXXXXXXXXXXXXXXXXXXXXXXXXXXXXXXXXXXXXXXX
XXXXXXXXXXXXXXXXXXXXXXXXXXXXXXXXXXXXXXXXXXXXXXXXXXXXXXXXXXXXXXXXX
XXXXXXXXXXXXXXXXXXXXXXXXXXXXXXXXXXXXXXXXXXXXXXXXXXXXXXXXXXXXXXXXX
XXXXXXXXXXXXXXXXXXXXXXXXXXXXXXXXXXXXXXXXXXXXXXXXXXXXXXXXXXXXXXXXX

XXXXXXXXXXXXXXXXXXXXXXXXXXXXXXXXXXXXXXXXXXXXXXXXXXXXXXXXXXXXXXXXX
XXXXXXXXXXXXXXXXXXXXXXXXXXXXXXXXXXXXXXXXXXXXXXXXXXXXXXXXXXXXXXXXX
XXXXXXXXXXXXXXXXXXXXXXXXXXXXXXXXXXXXXXXXXXXXXXXXXXXXXXXXXXXXXXXXX
XXXXXXXXXXXXXXXXXXXXXXXXXXXXXXXXXXXXXXXXXXXXXXXXXXXXXXXXXXXXXXXXX

XXXXXXXXXXXXXXXXXXXXXXXXXXXXXXXXXXXXXXXXXXXXXXXXXXXXXXXXXXXXXXXXX
XXXXXXXXXXXXXXXXXXXXXXXXXXXXXXXXXXXXXXXXXXXXXXXXXXXXXXXXXXXXXXXXX
XXXXXXXXXXXXXXXXXXXXXXXXXXXXXXXXXXXXXXXXXXXXXXXXXXXXXXXXXXXXXXXXX

            (complimentary closing)     XXXXXXXXXXXXXXX


                    (signature line)    XXXXXXXXXXXXXXX

    XXX:xxx(typist identification)
    XXXXXXXXXXX        (enclosure line)
```

THE REFERENCE RESUME COVER LETTER

You are about to join the ranks of jobgetters who use personalized, targeted reference letters to obtain immediate recognition by employers.

You've probably been advised not to attach a reference letter to your resume, or to give the names of your references until after the interview and when a job offer is likely.

That's because most jobseekers use the wrong *kind* of reference letter, and use it the wrong *way*. Let's rewrite the standard one so it will supercharge your search and generate your job.

---

57. Don't attach a reference letter to a resume going to the personnel department.

If you've read *any* of my books, you've got this rule indelibly etched in your memory. It's in all of them. Personnelers consider cover letters just one more piece of paper to shuffle. They're too busy to read them. The name of the writer and the gist of the contents are meaningless. At best, you've wasted the paper. At worst, you've wasted the interview.

---

58. Toss "To whom it may concern" letters into the trash.

This is the way reference letters begin. That's why they don't budge a job judge. You know the type: photocopied so many

times it's useless; written long ago by someone far away—
transferred to that great job in the sky.

If read at all, the letter just creates doubt about your
credibility. In some cases, it even contains wording inconsistent
from your resume.

59. Develop position power.

I discussed the elements of positioning in *The Perfect Job
Reference*:

> Marketeers always think about *positioning* a product or
> service. You have a service (your skills) and a product (you) to
> sell. To position you into the perfect position, you must
> position them correctly. It's nothing more than positioning
> yourself for the perfect position.

> What are the ingredients of a positioning letter? The letter
> should position its writer as an authority, be directed to the
> person with the proper position within the proper company,
> and be written to position you as an indispensable product
> with an incredible service.

> Presto![30]

60. Select preference references.

Chapters 3 and 4 discussed in detail the kinds of professional and
personal contacts to select as references—and how to cultivate
them. A preference reference fits any one of the following key
characteristics:

- The reference knows the recipient of the letter.
- The reference knows someone else the recipient knows.
- The reference is someone who, by reputation, is known
  to the recipient of the letter.

- The reference is someone whose letterhead and title will attract the recipient's attention or give credibility to the statements—and to you.

The writer of the letter should hold an equal or superior position to the recipient. An exception might be when the letter is written by a former employee who has a good relationship with his or her former boss. Another exception might be when the reference is on good terms with a higher level executive from another company whom he or she met at a conference.

61. Increase your "know-*who*."

As I stated in *The Perfect Job Reference*:

> Targeting the letter is the second essential element of positioning. When you contacted all your references, you advertised your availability. Many will have said, "Gee, I know _____, who's in charge of manufacturing (accounting/customer service/management information systems) at _____ company. Maybe I can put you in touch with him."

> Never refuse an offer like that. If your references don't offer, ask. Even if none can give you a push or a pull, perhaps they know someone who can.

> Consider the case of "Judy," who knew how to generate respectable reference representation.

>> Judy was stalled in her job as a writer of programming manuals for a small East Coast software manufacturer. She had been with the company for three years and had been promoted to supervisor of her department of four writers and a technical editor.

>> Although her undergraduate degree was in computer science, she'd studied at night to complete an MBA with an emphasis in marketing. Judy believed that her education, combined with her knowledge of user needs,

prepared her for a marketing manager position. But her company had only one such position, and it didn't look like it would be vacant soon.

So, Judy decided to review her contacts to find a few superstars that could become super-references. She wanted them to supercharge her into a bigger company where she could maximize her marketing training.

She decided on:

"Judd," a former coworker, who left to start a small software company. Although Judd's company only had a few products, one of them had recently been successful and was getting loads of industry attention. Judd's letterhead read "Justin Davis, President, Specialized Software Corporation" with a prestigious Los Angeles address.

Then there was "Elizabeth," a marketing manager of computer peripherals whom Judy had met at a conference; and

"Dr. William Dutton," an adjunct faculty member at the graduate school of business where Judy had studied, a former government official, and the Director of competitive intelligence for a defense manufacturing company. Judy took Dr. Dutton's course in competitive intelligence and business marketing. They became friends and she even helped him prepare a manuscript.

Judy's three principal references had a wealth of contacts in the software marketing business who could help her target marketing directors of manufacturers. The letters they wrote to introduce her and direct attention to her resume won her interview after interview. She had four reference-influenced offers, and today she's rapidly climbing the marketing ladder at one of the world's biggest software manufacturers.

Your story can be just that simple, its ending just that sweet. Even if you don't know any highly placed officials or company presidents, *somewhere* among your professional and personal contacts is *someone* (and another, and another) who will write a credible cover letter to get your resume read, your interview set, and your job offered.[31]

The following example of a perfect reference letter is among those in *The Perfect Job Reference.*[32]

The reference writing this letter and the "referee" are managers in different divisions of the same company. Note how the reference subtly reminds the referee of a past favor.

American Foods Company
2204 Mercantile Building • Chicago • Illinois 60626
(312) 974-0700

Angela P. Edwards, Director
Market Research

April 3, 19__

Margaret O. Blaine, Product Manager
Convenience Foods Division
American Foods Company
1667 Commonwealth Avenue
Boston, Massachusetts 02210

Re: Amanda F. Harston Reference

Dear Marge:

I hope all is going well with your new product launch. Last
November, when my department gave you that revised market
research you needed, you asked me to let you know if you
could return the favor. Well, now you can.

My associate and friend, Amanda Harston, is applying for
the assistant product manager position that opened at the
breakfast division of American. In addition to great
credentials, Amanda has the energy, insight, and dedication
needed to be an outstanding assistant product manager.

As the enclosed resume shows, Amanda recently enhanced her
ten years' experience in product marketing at XYZ, Inc.,
with an MBA from Bentley College. She graduated with high
honors in spite of a 60-hour-a-week job that required 70
percent travel. Although she has moved up steadily at XYZ,
now that she has solid experience and graduate credentials,
she'd like a larger environment.

I know John Lawson, who is hiring for this position, will
interview Amanda if the request comes from you. It won't be
a waste of time. In fact, John will probably feel he owes
you a favor once he meets Amanda. Please pass her resume
along to him; she'll call John for an interview by the end
of the week.

Thanks in advance for your assistance.

                                        Best regards,

                                        Angela P. Edwards

APE:sae
Enclosure: Amanda Harston resume

88

YOUR RESUME COVER LETTER

You must discipline yourself to fit your *entire* profile into a one-page, focused resume. Several separate resumes if you like, but only one page each. Write *more* and you risk being read *less*. Write in generalities and you won't directly hit the target.

Specific aspects of your background that relate directly to the target job should be mentioned in the cover letter. Be honest, not modest.

The perfect cover letter shows how your unique combination of character, skill, and experience makes you the perfect candidate for the job. A cover letter for your resume expands and customizes it. The letter can explain an employment gap or illuminate an area of your experience to turn that printed page into an 8 1/2-by-11-inch portrait. The more you know about a position in advance, the better your cover letter will be.

The resume cover letter must follow all the style rules in Tip 52. It must be no more than one page long, in block format, easy to read, concise, direct, and upbeat.

As for the content, study your target jobs and employers to learn what you have that they need and want. Then prepare a few riveting paragraphs that will get you an interview.

62. Don't attach a cover letter to a resume going to the human resources department.

I covered this in *Jeff Allen's Best: The Resume*. Overworked personnel types will just see it as one more piece of paper to shuffle. It may "cover" your resume for good.

63. Target your cover letter to a decision maker.

Always get a name. Aiming at a target is the only way to score an interview.

Don't send cover letters "To whom it may concern." If you have the name of a department, but not a person in that department with the authority to hire, don't bother with a cover letter.

64. Learn about the position before you write each letter.

If possible, talk to the decision maker on the telephone briefly to learn more about the position. That way, your customized cover letter will show you're custom made for the job. Your name will be remembered from the call, too.

Study the cover letter example on the next page from *The Perfect Job Reference*. [33]

15587 Russell Street
Greenville, South Carolina 29602

December 5, 19__

Abigail N. Hardesty
Director of Human Resources
Quality Furniture Manufacturers, Inc.
1500 Magnolia Boulevard
Charleston, South Carolina 29401

Re: Third Shift Production Manager Position

Dear Ms. Hardesty:

Your advertisement in the most recent edition of the Sunday Star Ledger called for a seasoned production manager to handle third-shift operations at your Durham, North Carolina, plant.

The enclosed resume reflects that I am well qualified for the position, with over 25 years furniture manufacturing experience. After graduation from high school, I began as an equipment operator and progressed through scheduling, purchasing, and inventory control to my current position as Production Manager of the first shift at Rosewood Furniture's Greenville plant. The challenge of managing Quality's much larger operation in Durham ignited my interest.

The "minimum educational requirements" specified in your ad were a Bachelor's Degree in business administration, manufacturing management, or its equivalent. When I began my career in 1964, a college education was not a prerequisite for rising through the manufacturing ranks. Through extension study and "on-the-job training," I have gained experience in all facets of the production environment. In fact, it is probably equivalent to several college degrees.

Rotating shift schedules have hampered my ability to attend all of the night classes for a degree, but I have managed to accumulate 65 credits toward a Bachelor of Science in Administration with a concentration in Manufacturing Management, and I intend to keep working until I've completed it.

I'll telephone you within the next week to set a convenient meeting date.

Very truly yours,

Thomas Y. Crowell

THE BROADCAST LETTER

A broadcast letter (solicitation letter) shotguns information about your attributes using the ammunition of a third-party testimonial. Unlike the reference cover letter discussed earlier, it is not personal to the "referee." Rather, a reference with impressive credentials writes a letter about you aimed at a group of senior executives.

Recruiters have used broadcast letters for years because they're a proven technique for placing candidates. When a respected colleague writes one and you mass-mail it directly, the results are even more effective.

It's a direct-mail approach with telephone follow-up. Professional marketeers call this "phone-mail," and it doubles—even triples—the results from direct mail alone.

You're not just looking for a job. You're running a campaign for office—a campaign to get you more money, prestige, and career fulfillment. Follow the methods that marketing pros use. They're the ones *self*-marketing pros use, too.

I discussed the benefits of direct-mail in *The Perfect Job Reference:*

> The proof of direct mail effectiveness fills your mailbox every day. The increase in the volume of direct mail over the past few years is astonishing. With the capacity of computer databases to locate, store, and retrieve information on everyone based upon every possible profile and preference, focused direct mail is a multibillion-dollar-a-year industry.
>
> Direct mail *works* because it is targeted. Unlike a commercial broadcast or advertising space, a direct mail message does

not compete with other advertisers for attention. If it gets to
the interested party, and it gets opened, it gets from one to
four minutes of the potential customer's undivided attention. This is more than any media advertising provides. That
translates into more sales.

Direct mail is also the most scientific, controllable, and cost-
effective method. A direct-mail jobseeker marketing campaign outperforms any you-against-the-world, one-step-at-a-
time approach to the job market. A phone/mail campaign
leverages your time and gets your name in front of decision
makers faster. In your case, it's not only going to get your
name in front of the decision makers, but your *face* in front
of them as well. From there, yours will be the new face on
Placement Place.[34]

The format you will use for this letter is identical to the
"look" described in Tip 52. But, since the same letter is going to
many "targets," you will have to omit personal "hooks."

65. Select your very best reference.

Select a "broadcaster" whose name or position will generate the
most excitement. It should be someone sincerely interested in
your success. You can collaborate to develop a reference cover
letter suitable for framing (along with a picture of you in your
new job).

That broadcaster should know how to motivate the movers
and shotgun the shakers.

66. Don't make your broadcast letter look like a mass-mailer.

Do not use "To whom it may concerns" photocopied onto copy
paper. Rather, follow the advice I gave in *The Perfect Job Reference*:

Each letter should be on high-quality (at least 24-pound) bond paper. The reference's letterhead, with raised type and watermark, is the best look for your letter.

If you have access to a word processor with a mail-merge program and a letter-quality printer, prepare originals on the reference's letterhead. A less effective way is to have an original typed neatly, and photocopy it on his or her letterhead. Then type in the name and address of each target. They should line up exactly as if they belonged there. Type the addresses on the same typewriter as the one used for the letter.

If the reference cannot supply you with 50 or more sheets of letterhead, you will have to resort to photocopies—but make sure they are on good, 24-pound *white* bond paper! It copies best, and the target may do a little internal mass mailing for you.

All letters should be signed individually by the reference. Envelopes should be typed individually, don't use a typed label.

This is personal correspondence, even if you do take some shortcuts to save time (and keep your reference happy). Think about your own reaction to mail solicitations. Which do you open first—the envelopes that look personalized or the ones that are obviously mass mailed?[35]

67.   Present the content for broad appeal.

The content should be just as sincere, measured, and factual as in all cover letters—but it must be convincing to more people. You have only a few seconds to capture the readers' attention. They're not consciously looking for anyone—yet.

They'll look at the letterhead first. If that interests them, next they'll glance down at the signature and read any "P.S." that appears below it. (Direct-mail pros pack their hardest sell into the P.S.). Finally, if they are still interested, they'll read the opening paragraph.

Each element of your letter must captivate your readers enough to go on. If they get to the opening paragraph, it has to be a real zinger to keep them reading.

Study this better broadcast letter example (shown on the following page) from *The Perfect Job Reference:*[36]

Henry V. Tattersall, III
Chief Financial Officer

January 15, 19__

Edgar O. Winston
Chief Financial Officer
General Investors Group
1200 Park Avenue
New York, New York 10011

Re: Joel M. Adams Reference

Dear Mr. Winston:

As Chief Financial Officers of multinational companies, you
and I know how important the internal audit process is to
our financial stability. But talented, skilled, effective
audit managers are almost impossible to find.

My associate, Joel Adams, is one of them. A 20-year veteran
of multinational audit management with direct responsibil-
ity to the CFO, Mr. Adams uses his keen understanding of
the audit process to develop solutions to complex financial
problems. His enclosed resume will illuminate his record at
Wharton and his ability as an audit manager.

Mr. Adams reported directly to me in my former position as
CFO at Amalgamated Industries. Amalgamated's acquisition by
U.F.O. has placed him into the job market. I'm letting you
know he is available in the event that you could benefit
from the expertise of a highly qualified audit manager.

Please speak with Mr. Adams when he calls. I am confident
it will be mutually beneficial.

Sincerely,

Henry V. Tattersall, III

P.S. Please let your secretary know that Joel Adams will be
telephoning your office for an appointment within the week.

HVT:meg
Enclosure: Joel M. Adams resume

68. Research your list of targets.

Through the kind of exhaustive industry research I described in Chapter 1, "Get Ready to Get Interviews," you can develop a list of names and contact information for key decision makers in companies where you'd like to work. In your networking calls, ask for names to add to the list.

In addition to traditional sources of information on companies, telephone sleuthing will turn up the information you need. The most effective method is to call and identify yourself as a consultant working for a client (you are—you). This is known as "doing yourself a favor."

Say that your client provides services to that industry (he or she does), and you would like the names of key personnel involved in acquiring your client's type of services. Know the names of the positions you are targeting: Marketing Director, Management Information Systems Manager, Production Supervisor, and so forth. Be businesslike and time-conscious. Sound like you know what you're doing. You do.

69. Play the direct-mail numbers game.

A well-developed and properly executed direct-mail promotion can expect, at best, to get a 1.5 percent response. That's why mailings of one million pieces are commonplace.

No, you don't have to mail a million letters. That's a cannon, not a shotgun. But you should mail from 50 to 100. In a direct-mail campaign alone (without phone follow-up), you can expect only one or two targets to respond.

But in the phone-mail campaign, you call every one of the recipients by the end of the week when they receive your letter. From mailing 100 letters, you can expect between 5 and 10 to arrange an interview. Otherwise, they'll generally give you the name of someone else who might be interested.

70. Record, track, and follow-up each cover letter you send.

Regardless of the type of letter you use to get an interview scheduled, keep careful track of what you sent when and where. Then follow up! (The form on the next page will facilitate this.)

71. Time the arrival of your letters.

This is crucial. Monday morning usually brings more mail and messages. Fridays are for finishing and firing. Your letter should arrive on a Tuesday or Wednesday. By first-class mail, allow two to three days for delivery. Mail local letters on Monday, out-of-state letters on Friday.

72. Call within two days of your letter's arrival.

Once again, the Monday/Friday rule applies. If your letter arrived Tuesday or Wednesday, call on Thursday, between 9:00 and 10:00 A.M. (before the day's meetings start) or after 4:00 p.m. (when things have slowed down).

   If you don't get through the first time, don't give up. If you do get through, talk to the target. Ask to meet with him or her personally. If he or she declines, don't hang up without getting the name of another decision maker.

73. Follow the follow-up telephone call script.

The script on page 100 from *The Perfect Job Reference*[37] can be customized to each cover letter situation. This particular script was used for follow-up to a broadcast letter. All of your cover letters should get the same telephone treatment—fast.

Career Campaign Follow-Up

Date Sent	Type of Letter (or Resume Only)	Addressee & Company	Signer	Called On	Results

Version 1 (Target Is in His or Her Office and Interested):

Candidate: Hello, this is Joel Adams. My colleague, Mr. Tattersall, wrote to Mr. Winston about me. I'm calling to follow up on that letter. Is he available?

Secretary: One moment, I'll see if he can take your call, Mr. Adams. (Pause) Yes, Mr. Winston is available. I'll connect you now.

Target: Henry Winston.

Candidate: I'm Joel Adams, the audit manager our mutual friend Mr. Tattersall wrote about.

Target: Yes, Mr. Adams, I got the letter. Very impressive resume, too. I would like to talk to you some time next week. I'll give you back to my secretary and she can arrange it.

Candidate: Thank you. I look forward to meeting you.

Version 2 (Target Is in His or Her Office, No Position Available):

Candidate: Hello, this is Joel Adams. My colleague, Mr. Tattersall, wrote to Mr. Winston about me. I'm calling to follow up on that letter. Is he available?

Secretary: One moment, I'll see if he can take your call, Mr. Adams. (Pause) Yes, Mr. Winston is available. I'll connect you now.

Target: Henry Winston.

Candidate: I'm Joel Adams, the audit manager our mutual friend Mr. Tattersall wrote about.

Target: Hello, Mr. Adams. Yes, I received Henry's letter and your resume. I was very impressed with your credentials. However, I am sorry that I can't offer you any encouragement at the present time.

Candidate: I'm disappointed, too. I've long admired your operation. You have one of the finest reputations in the industry. Perhaps you know of someone else I could talk to?

Target: Yes, as a matter of fact, I do . . .

Version 3 (Target Is in a Meeting):

Candidate: Hello, this is Joel Adams. My colleague, Mr. Tattersall, wrote to Mr. Winston about me. I'm calling to follow up on that letter. Is he available?

Secretary: One moment, I'll see if he can take your call, Mr. Adams. (Pause) No, I'm sorry, sir, Mr. Winston is in a meeting and can't be disturbed.

Candidate: I understand, I'll be happy to call Mr. Winston at his convenience, if you'll tell me when he'll have a few minutes to talk.

Secretary: Hmm, let me see. He's scheduled for meetings all day, but he'll be in his office between 9 and 10 tomorrow.

Candidate: I'll call him at 9 tomorrow. Thank you.

Be consistent and reliable in your calls. Be sure to call back when you say you will. Your performance as a jobseeker signals the prospective employer about what to expect of you as an employee.

---

74. Conduct a campaign you can keep up with.

Don't overload yourself. If you can't keep up with your follow-up phoning, your phone-mail campaign will fail. If you're sending 100 letters, don't schedule them all to arrive on the same Tuesday, because you'll never make 100 follow-up phone calls on Thursday of the same week. You don't want your name to have faded from their memory by the time you call.

You can only make about 25 follow-up phone calls a day and still sound enthusiastic. Therefore, your phone-mail campaign will take about a month to complete. In the meantime, you'll be going on interviews and feeling confident as your jobgetting skills improve.

Be realistic. If you're still working and you'll never get time away from your work to make 25 personal calls, reduce the number of letters you send each week and extend your campaign over a longer period of time.

Sending out and calling the recipients of 50 to 100 letters should net you 5 to 10 interviews. The average applicant gets one offer for every three interviews, so you should have at least three offers by the end of your campaign. And these results are realized from only one technique in your interview-getting campaign! There's more to come!

Next Up: The Classifieds

In Chapter 6, I'll give you a clear look at classified advertising, including sources few jobseekers consider. We'll discuss what it can't and won't do, then what you can make it do for you.

Chapter

6

Using and Choosing the Classifieds

If you're using the classified ads to see what's out there, this section offers help with the "help wanted." Although employment classified advertising fills page after page of every local daily newspaper in the country—and sometimes several whole sections of each one on Sunday—it's anything but what it appears to be: an organized listing of jobs available and the specifications for the positions. More often than not, what employers *really* want is "classified information"—the last place you'll find it is in the ads.

Further, only 15 percent of available jobs are ever advertised. The people who get jobs from them know the games employers play with the classifieds. Follow these techniques, and you'll be one of them.

75. Read between the lines.

As I told readers in *How to Turn an Interview into a Job*, there are five types of ads:

1. THE ONES THAT DON'T SAY WHAT THEY MEAN (25 PERCENT).

Confusing words are usually the sign of a confused mind. This occurs most often because the interviewer is rushing to meet the advertising deadline. The salesperson in the newspaper classified office is equally frantic, and the result reads like an eye chart.

A quarter of the classified advertisements are consistently unintelligible, except for the title (which may be inaccurate). A telephone call is particularly effective in these cases, because the interviewer may not have ascertained what he is looking for. An artful conversation can pace and lead effectively. It is like picking wallpaper: the first one you see will often be the one you choose. This is when you are most impressionable and when the image becomes fixed in your mind. For this reason, an immediate interview is imperative to lock in your image as a personification of the applicant to be hired.

"No" often means "maybe," so this approach can be frustrating. However, it may be the closest you ever come to customizing your job *and* your salary.

2. THE ONES THAT DON'T MEAN WHAT THEY SAY (35 PERCENT).

This advertisement appears most often and is difficult to identify with any accuracy. Many are intentionally misleading. Others are just looking for someone else. . . .

Intentionally misleading ads are designed to bait and switch you into another position or identify you as someone seeking employment. These are the ones that seem to be "written for you" and, of course, are designed to draw the largest response possible. Glamour jobs in media and fashion industries are often featured, as are "lucrative" positions in management, marketing, and personnel administration.

Although there may be some ways you can spot these ads, I don't recommend that you attempt to do so. As with interviews, it is just another chance, and you owe it to yourself to take it. You don't have to take a job you don't want, so let them attempt to switch you all they like. . . .

Inadvertently misleading advertisements contain latent ambiguities that were not obvious to the interviewer when the ad was placed. You probably will be screened out long before the appointment, since the interviewer's error will become painfully obvious to him rather quickly. This is a lesson most interviewers learn fast.

If your qualifications fit the hidden agenda, you may never discover the ambiguity. So be it.

3. THE ONES THAT DON'T KNOW WHAT THEY'RE SAYING (25 PERCENT)

These well-intentioned folks are the ones who take open requisitions and recite them in the advertisements. It takes a lot more than buzz words to really understand the specialized jobs in many companies. It takes an understanding of the personal characteristics necessary to perform the function.

Fully a quarter of all the ads you will see contain misstatements or omit essential duties. This is just because the interviewer didn't do his homework, or is trying to assure the powers that be that he is doing everything possible to find suitable applicants.

You can't really do much about this, but you stand an excellent chance of passing the initial interview by studying the advertisement carefully and using it as your theme. After all, you need to know only slightly more than the interviewer about the technical part of the job.

You'll eventually find that the supervisor who wrote the "rec" probably answered an ad just like it when he was hired!

4. THE ONES THAT SAY IT AND MEAN IT (15 PERCENT)

Yes, there are some straight talkers out there. But, alas, their seriousness means they have probably already gone through their application files, posted the job on the bulletin boards, offered "bounties" to other employees for referrals, researched wage and salary data, placed job orders, and have otherwise been disciplined in their target practice.

Your chances of getting hired probably will depend upon rigorous, objective criteria, but understanding the advertisement thoroughly and emphasizing those attributes will improve them. These ads appear only 15 percent of the time, but the employers are worth pursuing. They know what they're looking for.

5. THE ONES THAT DON'T ADMIT THEY SAID IT.

Ah, yes, those little cowards hiding inside newspaper reply boxes, able to eat their lunches. You know they're out there, but only one in twenty ever sends a reply. You're always sure it will be *your* boss. . . .[38]

As for the last item, if you're still employed, play it safe. Don't reply. If you're unemployed, take the chance. Just when you run out of stamps, someone will call.

76. Don't limit yourself to local advertising.

You can read the ads in your local papers, and send for copies of the locals from where you might relocate, but they're not the only source. There are several national job listings that appear weekly, the best of which is: *National Business Employment Weekly* [420 Lexington Avenue, New York, NY 10170 (212) 808-6796]. It's a compilation of all the job listings that appeared in *The Wall Street Journal* that week.

Check with your public library to see if they have a subscription.

77. Get creative—classifieds aren't the only advertisements.

There are plenty of job openings advertised in other sections of papers and magazines. Just because they don't appear under the heading "classified" doesn't mean they're top secret. Uncovering clues takes a willingness to read (actually "scan"—it doesn't take a magnifying glass to find clues).

Watch for information on mergers, acquisitions, buyouts, businesses for sale, reorganizations, layoffs, and even downsizes. Companies going through upheaval tend to ignore employees and are easily infatuated with strangers bearing magic wands. If "luck" is when preparation meets opportunity, look for luck in the news.

Speaking of nontraditional "advertising," *The Executive Moonlighter*, by David Eyler, gave aspiring consultants information that can help jobseekers as well:

> The economy's largest purchaser of goods and services is the U.S. Government, making it a source worthy of investigation by any moonlighting consultant. . . . The most reliable printed source of government opportunities is the *Commerce Business Daily*. It is available in libraries, or you can have it delivered to your door. The address is: Superintendent of Documents, Government Printing Office, Washington, D.C. 20402-9371 or you can call 202-783-3238 with your Visa or MasterCard.

> [I]t is . . . "A daily list of U.S. Government procurement invitations, contract awards, subcontracting leads, sales of surplus property, and foreign business opportunities." That covers a lot of territory and many of the entries call for complex services that will only be delivered by huge defense contractors and the like. On the other hand, there are countless listings that hold potential for performance by individuals or small organizations with expertise in a broad spectrum of areas. . . .

> Another useful application for the *Commerce Business Daily* for the moonlighting consultant [or the motivated jobseeker] is the section entitled "Contract Awards." By reading it under your area of interest, it is possible to identify the companies that are *winning* government contracts. It will tell you the dollar value of the award and give you the name and address of the recipient. In many cases, it will be a major company whose name you recognize. In other instances, it will be the names of companies that maintain offices and limited permanent staff for the purposes of identifying and securing government contracts. They then hire. . . . There is nothing illegal about this. Many are listed with government

agencies and have the track records of successful performance essential in securing these multimillion-dollar con-
tracts. . . .

A little bit of diligence in finding such a listing in all the chaff
of the general publication can pay rich dividends. But not if
you fail to persist in getting on the telephone or into a
directory and determining the name of a relevant contact
within that firm. Get past the receptionist, and find your
professional counterpart. If you are an engineer, a program-
mer, a technical writer, or whatever, probe until you are on
the line and talking with that person. See if he or she needs
your contribution and supply your resume immediately with
a cover letter citing your telephone conversation and thank-
ing them for their interest in you. It works![39]

Using this creative approach, you'll be expanding the scope
of your interviewing and your career opportunities.

78. Time the arrival of your responses.

The bigger the ad, the greater the number of responses it usually
generates. This diminishes the probability of being considered
favorably. Almost nobody is hired from the first "batches" of
resumes. Resist the temptation—it's not a placement race.

Time your resume to arrive the following Tuesday, Wednesday or Thursday. (Wednesday or Thursday if Monday is a holi-
day.)

Depending on the distance your first-class envelope must
travel, factor sufficient mailing time. Mail to the same or a
nearby city on Monday morning for Tuesday arrival. Drop it in
the mail on Friday or Saturday to more distant points.

79. Write your own classified.

If there's nothing you see that you like in the classifieds, write
your own ad and place it in the "positions wanted" category.
Concise, clear copy with an emphasis on achievement and what

you can do for the employer could get your telephone to ring. It's expensive, though, so write tight.

Don't say too much—three or four lines is plenty. Place it in the middle of the week when the competition is lighter. You might even invest in your own "classified display" ad (a boxed ad like the major employers use) to improve its visual impact.

Next Up: Getting Placement Help

Getting a job is a do-it-yourself proposition for everyone. Now that you know the self-marketing strategies for getting interviews on your own, it's time for me to sing *Welcome to My World.*

The world of the recruiter—the *placer.* Marketability turns "applicants" into "candidates." Now, you'll be one of them, sought by recruiters. People like you make the placement planet go 'round.

Chapter

7

Help from
Placement People

If you're like most jobseekers, the terms "executive recruiter," "personnel consultant," "placement counselor," "executive search firm," "personnel service," and "employment agency" confuse you.

Once you know who these placement people are, how they operate, and how they think, you can leverage your job search. You'll know how to select the best in the business, and get them working their national networks to find you the best opportunities.

80. Recruit an executive recruiter.

"Executive recruiter" is synonymous with the following terms:

- Professional recuiter
- Management recruiter
- Technical recruiter
- Executive search consultant
- Professional search consultant
- Management search consultant
- Technical search consultant

All translate into the same job jungle jargon: "headhunter." They're more interested if *they* find *you* first. If you call them, the thrill of the chase is gone. You have to get their attention because you're marketable—placeable. That usually involves having

your name given to them by someone else or getting publicity for
an innovation, seminar presentation, or publication.

Executive recruiters are paid by the employer ("client").
Only about five percent are actually paid anything to identify and
recruit qualified candidates for a specific position. The words
"retained" and "client" are used. But the probability is 95 percent that the recruiter has either no job order at all or one for a
contingency fee, nonexclusive job order.

They're probably competing with several other outside
recruiters (and the employer itself) to fill the position as quickly
as possible. The placement fee is usually one percent per
thousand dollars of the candidate's projected first-year
compensation. It's among the toughest jobs behind any desk. The
longer they look, the less they make, so they're interested in
getting a job filled fast. In their world, there's not much time for
social work.

Some recruiters are independent, operating from a desk in
their home, while others work for organizations of various sizes.
The average office has 3 desks, but some have almost 50. They
thrive on the chase (identification) and kill (placement). They are
quick of flight, have a positive attitude, sensitive faculties, and
a keen sense of timing. They truly are "headhunters" who know
that job jungle instinctively.

Search businesses are often owned by management, technical, and sales executives from various industries. More and more
of them are specializing in certain occupations, industries, or
geographic areas.

Several of the larger national recruiting organizations are
owned by major corporations. Most of these have developed a
franchise system. Office managers and recruiters are compen-
sated based on the placement fees received, or "cash in." Some
(particularly the refugees from human resource departments) use
big words. Most know the ropes and the rules. You have to
impress them before you'll become a "send-out" to their clients.
They're only as good as their last placement.

The techniques we've covered will have you being "sent
out" to interviews regularly. You may even be considered an

"MPC" (most placeable candidate). If so, they'll "run with you," using your credentials to interest the employer in hiring.

Then use the techniques in the third book in this series, *Jeff Allen's Best: Win the Job*, to get hired.

Recruiters are successful because they know where the action is. They dig deep and discover the corporate cultures and internal politics of their clients. They know which companies are flying into the future, and which are peddling in the past. They know when promotions create job opportunities and when key employees are about to leave.

They know the environments that incubate innovation and those that crush creativity. They know which companies reward excellence with high pay, and those who just "buy" employees.

Headhunters are in the intelligence business. They have contacts who smuggle company newsletters to them so they can identify potential recruits.

If you want headhunters to hawk you, walk and talk where they stalk. One way is through coverage in your company newsletter. "Editors" (personnelers) never have enough non-sense to fill those pages, and ghost write most of the articles. They're grateful for anyone who'll lend their name and picture. It makes them look like they're keeping morale up in the ozone. Then you can anonymously send the newsletter to local hunters. It's called "bait," placed there by the quarry. Include other press clippings if you have them.

Executive recruiters tend to be clustered in major urban areas, and can be found in the *Yellow Pages* under any of the headings in the previous list.

Also, check your network to see if anyone you know has a recommendation. If that fails to produce a name, call several firms and ask which recruiters "work" your specialty.

Send your resume, reference letters, and press releases to these recruiters with a cover letter. Then follow up to see who is most interested. If you find yourself chasing after a recruiter, you're chasing in place. There's not the remotest chance you'll be presented by him or her. You're too available. You don't know the placement plays—or even the score.

81. Enlist an employment agency.

Employment agencies ("personnel agencies") usually place employees from entry level through mid-management. Some place up to top management. If your search is in the $30,000 annual salary range or less, true recruiters won't even talk to you—but employment agencies will.

It won't cost you anything but well-spent time. In recent years, more than 90 percent of agencies have changed their fee policies from applicant-paid (fee) to employer-paid (free).

Consultants ("commissioned matchmakers") who work the desks are among the brightest, most positive, helpful human beings in the working world. Their placements occur more frequently, so they're used to a larger inventory of candidates and job orders than recruiters. They handle interruptions with ease, and will assist you confidentially if you prefer.

The great strength of employment agencies is their "street smarts," unpretentiousness, and flexibility to serve candidates and employers. Most fill temporary as well as permanent job orders (where they are the employer), increasing the number of options for jobseekers.

If you've avoided employment agencies until now because you thought their inhabitants had a communicable disease, you're the one who needs a cure. Make an appointment and go in thoroughly prepared as you would for a job interview.

You'll find them in the *Yellow Pages* under "Employment Agencies," "Personnel Agencies," "Personnel Services," "Employment-Permanent," or similar headings.

82. Try temporary employment services.

Temporary employment services ("temp services") interview applicants in a variety of specialties. Those who meet their specifications are hired, then placed in client companies for as short as a day or as long as a year. The service collects a fee from the client, then pays the "temp" an hourly rate that is somewhat lower. The service collects all employee payroll deductions and pays employment taxes like any other employer. Some even offer health insurance benefits, paid vacations, and bonuses.

At one time, temporary services specialized in general labor or clerical jobs. But as employers recognize the high cost of carrying full-time employees on the payroll, they're using temps for interim assistance in everything from accounting to engineering.

Temporary assignments can be ideal for the serious job-seeker, because they offer an inside look at a company that classified ads—and even interviews—cannot. Once inside, temporary employees look just like permanent staffers. They make friends with coworkers, join them for breaks, and get the inside scoop on upcoming job openings.

The employer gets the opportunity to really know an employee before hiring him or her "direct," too. It's a "try before you buy" arrangement that benefits both parties. Maybe someday it'll be mandatory—like living together before you get married. If you'll lobby for it, I'll draft the law.

The temp services won't mind—they charge a "conversion fee" if the hire occurs before a certain time (usually 90 days).

83. Know the ins and outs of outplacement.

In *Surviving Corporate Downsizing*,[40] I noted that outplacement consultants can be spotted a mile away. They're the specialists who are paid to accompany human resourcers into termination interviews. They're well groomed and impeccably dressed, just like undertakers.

Many know a lot about severance benefits and the job market. All have protecting the employer as their highest priority. Assisting the employee is nice, too.

Among the services they provide to the downsized and displaced (at the employer's expense) are:

- Counseling with the employee and his of her family.
- Assessing the employee's job strengths and weaknesses.
- Identifying the employee's transferable knowledge and skills.
- Isolating suitable jobs.
- Developing a jobseeking strategy.
- Preparing letters and resumes.
- Target-mailing letters and resumes.
- Training in securing interviews. (You could train *them*, now!)
- Training for interviews and salary negotiation.

Employer-paid outplacement services vary in structure and duration, but all generally include an assessment of the outplaced employee's strengths and job opportunities. (They also include an assessment of the employer's liability for wrongful termination.)

If outplacement is available to you, take it; but don't rely on it as your only strategy. The outplacer's agenda only incidentally includes getting you hired. Yours only incidentally includes anything else.

If your employer offers a month of office space and use of a telephone, decline. It sounds nice, but it's demoralizing to see your former coworkers still at their jobs. Soon, you interpret every smile as an expression of pity. That doesn't help your mental preparation for career calisthenics.

84. Choose career counselors carefully.

The latest career consultants' con is to call themselves "individual outplacement firms." They use that title to confuse unsuspecting jobseekers and align themselves with the reputable, employer-paid segment of the industry.

These businesses (which historically call themselves "career consultants") offer services to help you find your own job. Vulnerable people pay $5,000, even $10,000, in advance. Many receive no more than books to read (mine, I hear), resumes, and "counseling" that does everything but get them a fulfilling job.

You can get a lot more than what these "counselors" or "consultants" "advise" in the *Jeff Allen's Best* series. The only difference is that they'll coach you personally. Too bad they can't prop you up during an interview.

Their value is in getting you *interviews*. If you can negotiate a fixed fee for every interview you accept, go for it. Then follow *Jeff Allen's Best: Win the Job* to get offers.

85. Connect with college placement services.

If you're about to graduate, get some dividends on those tuition payments by using your campus placement service. Find out when corporate recruiters will be on campus. You don't have to limit your interviews to the recruiters who come to your school or college. If you're graduating from the college of liberal arts, it won't hurt to inquire about appointments at the business school. Major corporations are recognizing that liberal arts majors have the human relations skills their business majors lack.

If you've been out of school for a while, reconnect with your campus placement office. There may be opportunities now. The staff may also have information about other, higher level openings at companies that don't recruit on campus. This is a version of networking, and it's a wide net too few people weave after they graduate.

86. Marshall your troops and organize the assault.

When working with the placement players, you have to make the rules of the game. Otherwise, they won't be able to help you as well. Follow the suggestions I gave in *Surviving Corporate Downsizing*:

> While you're employed, select no more than six placement services, furnish them with a current resume, and insist on:
>
> 1. *Only one consultant from each service,* preferably the person most knowledgeable about the jobs you desire.
> 2. *No calls at your office.* All interviews, including theirs, must be scheduled and conducted after working hours.
>
> Change services if you're not satisfied, but six is all you can comfortably handle on a part-time basis.
>
> If you decide to pursue the leads, interview scheduling must be rigidly and discreetly done. Extended lunch hours and too many "errands" pressure you unnecessarily and just increase your axe anxiety. If you want to cross over into active interviewing, do so on evenings, weekends, vacations, and "sick leave" time. In any case, you won't get a job offer when you're rushed. In fact, it's counterproductive.[41]

Next Up: Miscellaneous Strategies to Increase Interviews

Just in case, Chapter 8 offers a few final fail-safe techniques.

Chapter

8

Miscellaneous Techniques

This chapter contains the final proven producers of interviews.

87. Go on a job jungle safari.

One way to be attractive to a potential employer is to assume some of the risk of interviewing. That could mean paying the cost of travel and other expenses to interview.

There are various ways to do this economically. One way is to plan these journeys around already scheduled business trips. If you're now employed and have business trips coming up, research the job markets where you are going. Include cities that might be easy stopovers. Target employers and placement services there.

If you have control over your travel schedule, plan your trips for late in the week and take Friday or Saturday as personal time. You're probably traveling on regular coach airline tickets, so it's easy to change your return date without anyone knowing. Your only costs may be an extra night in a hotel, a few meals, and transportation. Maybe not even that—employers rarely question incidental weekend return expenses.

Do your phonework in advance. Weave your getwork network, make telephone contact with targets, send your resume with a cover letter, and follow up until you get an interview. Your "hook" is that you're "in the area on business" and it won't cost the employer anything to talk with you. But this is an opportunity that may never be repeated again, so they have to act fast!

Even if the companies have no immediate openings, it costs them nothing to discuss future possibilities. The more attractive you make yourself as a candidate, the more likely you will schedule an interview.

If you're not employed, or don't travel, you might have to schedule your own job jungle safari—and pay for it. Travel is surprisingly inexpensive if you fly "standby" and stay in no-frills motels. Select an area where you can develop several leads. Schedule a one-week trip. Then match targets with dates and arrange one morning and one afternoon interview per day. (No more—you'll start blowing them. I discuss why in *Jeff Allen's Best: Win the Job*.

Some airlines offer unlimited 30-day passes to all the cities they serve for less than a one-way coach ticket to any of those cities. They also cooperate with car rental and ground transportation services, so discounts are everywhere. When you're in an area, "close" interview appointments with, "I'm leaving the area tomorrow and we should meet before I go."

Whatever way you set up your safari, do it with sufficient planning to maximize the number of quality interviews in the time available.

88. Get your name in print.

In Chapter 7, I discussed the importance of publicity to get yourself noticed by headhunters. *Employers* notice, too. Get coverage in industry publications for something you've developed, written, or presented.

An article in a trade journal might deserve your reply. That could lead to publication, friendship with an editor, and additional opportunities to contribute.

Send your resume to the editors of *all* industry publications. The cover letter should highlight your expertise and offer to provide assistance whenever there's a story in your field. Your fee? Just a quote with "attribution."

Keep track of your press coverage for future use.

89.   Write your own newsletter.

If your job doesn't offer the opportunity to be profiled in the news, do it yourself. Write a newsletter in your specialty and send it to a target list of decision makers in other companies. Desktop publishing software and laser printers make it easy for you to produce a professional quality publication at home for minimal expense.

This strategy is particularly effective in occupations such as advertising, public relations, and accounting where there is so much new data daily. Careful reading and condensing of the news on a regular basis can be fun, too.

Develop a list of "advisors" for your publication among those executives, and ask their opinions when you write articles. They might also give you permission to print their names on your newsletter masthead under "professional advisors."

If you're not familiar with this field, there are many inexpensive "desktop publishing" courses available. Check with your local college for extension courses. Do it right, and you may even find your new career—right on your desktop!

90.   Conduct a public relations campaign.

If you're a highly paid executive, a public relations firm may be worth the investment. Burdette Bostwick mentioned in his book, *111 Proven Techniques and Strategies for Getting the Job Interview*:

> In the upper-income bracket you can employ your own public relations firm, paid tax-free, out of your own pocket. What can result from this? News releases, profiles, business stories, announcements, and all kinds of items in the print media, which, more frequently than one might think, welcome interesting information.
>
> In some instances, public relations executives can influence appointments to boards of directors.

Many business leaders gain attention without seeking it. If you are not one of those, let a public relations firm do some work for you if you can afford it. Done subtly, it can be very advantageous.[42]

Even if you're not earning a high income, public relations can work for you. If your present employer has a PR department, introduce yourself to someone there and ask how the department works. Whenever the opportunity arises, give them information about you, your activities, or your department to release to the press.

Finally, you can be your own press agent. If you're speaking at a seminar or have developed a new process, write your own press releases and send them to interested publications. Make sure your actions are approved by your employer, and be sure your employer gets credit when appropriate.

91. Use portfolio power.

Projects you've accomplished demonstrate your ability. Samples of it make excellent keys to open interview doors. This includes writing or artwork (published or unpublished), inventions, press clippings describing your accomplishments, or copies of research papers.

Assemble the portfolios and mail them to target decision makers. Follow up by phone and schedule a meeting. If your portfolio is extensive, write a letter describing your work, then call to set up a "presentation."

92. Audition via video.

In *Jeff Allen's Best: The Resume*, I devoted a chapter to video resumes and how to use them. They don't open interview doors unless they are exceptional.

A variation on the theme of video resumes is the video interview. In recent years, "video interview" businesses offer employers the ability to watch the tape before inviting the candidate to interview. You usually don't learn of this possibility until you contact an employer and someone refers you to the video interviewer in your area. The employer pays, although you can buy the tape, too.

If you're good at getting information on the phone, contact a video interview service in your area and ask what employers use them. Then contact the employer and suggest taping an interview.

93. Use expedited communications.

FAX machines, computer modems, mailgrams, E-mail, overnight delivery services, and other methods of expedited communication can be effective in getting your messages, cover letters, and resumes into the hands of decision makers.

Just avoid being too aggressive, desperate, or strange. Aggressive, desperate, strange people don't get interviews. Investigate the target job and decision maker, and use this strategy only if you're sure it will have a positive effect. It rarely does. The hiring process is a slow, committee-dominated, often-avoided activity.

You further your cause by talking with the hirer and advising him or her to expect the communication from you. You can also use this strategy if your initial calls and cover letters have gone unanswered. It won't get you hired, but it might get you attention.

94. Join the "advice squad."

In Chapter 2, "Telephone Techniques," I discussed "the consultant phone call." Setting yourself up as a consultant in your industry can have long-term job advantages.

Like temporary employment, which is not available to many executives, independent consulting affords an inside look at a company and what it needs. A consultant has the immediate advantage of being recognized as an "expert." Many have transferred to the payroll in client companies, with better jobs than the ones they left.

You'll need above-average knowledge of your field, good communication skills, business cards, and simple but professional brochures explaining your services. Then, a telephone, good grooming, and conservative business clothes will make you a card-carrying member of the "advice squad."

---

95. Moonlight into a daytime interview.

After-hours work in a similar or different field is a natural way to develop the contacts for interviews. David Eyler discussed how to do this in *The Executive Moonlighter*:

> The picture of the moonlighting worker as the struggling blue-collar guy who drags himself from one eight-hour shift to the next is no longer accurate. Today's moonlighter is just as likely to be a professional colleague who has found a way to extend his services to a market as yet untouched by his employer—perhaps by reaching beyond the geographic limits exploited by his company or maybe by choosing to provide a service that isn't even close to what he does for the firm that cuts his regular paycheck.[43]

Eyler's book describes ways to break into new endeavors from a desk in your own home, using the security of your present position and salary to cushion your landing into a new career. The contacts you make moonlighting become job leads.

People who make a successful transition from employed to self-employed are sought by employers after they become established in their businesses. Where were these offers when they were unhappily employed?

The phone doesn't ring unless you appear in demand. Get noticed for good things, and the world beats a path to your door.

By that time, it's too late to "go to work" again. You remember why it was called "work." Why they *paid* you to do it.

96. Find a niche.

If self-employment isn't appealing to you, become a specialist. Pay attention to trends, with your employer and others. Learn what they need before *they* know. Then present yourself as the "expert" who can do the job. You just need the confidence to communicate your ideas. Then you can customize your job description in accordance with your preferences.

97. Journey to job fairs.

These are usually held by employers in industries suffering labor shortages, such as nursing, data processing, and electronics. Companies who need skilled workers advertise these events in the classified ads.

If your skill is in demand, you might not be having trouble finding a job. But, have you found the best possible job? It's a buyer's market for your skills, and a fair becomes a self-service supermarket.

If you attend these fairs, travel alone. Dress and conduct yourself professionally. Take time to talk with (and listen to) company representatives. Leave a copy of your perfect resume. Get their names and complete addresses, and write follow-up letters the next day. If they call you for an interview, the chances of being hired are *80 percent*!

Even if you aren't in one of the "hot careers," attend the fair to network. Go with the goal of getting names of decision makers who could hire you. The company's on the move and more jobs will be opening. Get the names of the people who referred you, and mention them in your cover letter when you send your resume.

98. Connect at conventions.

Another excellent source of job leads are industry conventions. Attend as many as possible, even if you're only just "passively" looking. It's a great way to make contacts for future networking. Most of the people are there to advance their careers. The environment makes them far more receptive to meeting and greeting.

Get the exhibitor list in advance and request tickets to the functions held "above" the show floor—the receptions in hotel suites. If you live near a major city, call the convention bureau and ask for a list of upcoming trade shows.

It's an excellent way to look inside a different industry, too.

99. Volunteer your way to better pay.

Volunteer activities can boost your career. There's the opportunity to meet influential executives and community leaders. You can also develop and demonstrate your ability to a wide audience. Your active and visible volunteer role will get you noticed in the news, too.

Writing a grant proposal to help a nonprofit organization get government money creates another opportunity. A good "grant writer" can create a position for himself or herself as part of the proposal. Many volunteers labor for years out of love, and are then rewarded with paid leadership positions as the organization evolves.

100. Be calendar conscious.

As a rule, July and August are slower, as is the stretch from mid-November to mid-January. Scurrying college grads make it difficult to get noticed in June, and even to some extent September. That leaves the first five months of the year as optimum opportunity time. Mid-September through mid-November are second best.

That doesn't mean you should live your livelihood by the calendar. I got the best job of my career between Christmas and New Year's. Just don't take rejection during downtimes personally. They're the best times to weave your getwork network, prepare your perfect resume, write your cover letter, and target your search.

Conclusion

Select from these 100 techniques to organize your search. Follow up on every lead they produce, and track your progress so that you learn what works best for you.

Before you finish setting up your auditions, you'll be giving them. You need some acting lessons—fast. They're in my final book of this series, *Jeff Allen's Best: Win the Job.*

Best wishes for superstar success!

Endnotes

1. Allen, Jeffrey G., J.D., C.P.C., *How to Turn an Interview into a Job*. New York: Simon & Schuster, 1981, pp. 83–86.

2. Allen, Jeffrey G., J.D., C.P.C., *Surviving Corporate Downsizing*. New York: John Wiley & Sons, 1988, pp. 24–26.

3. Korda, Michael, *Power! How to Get It, How to Use It*. New York: Ballantine Books, 1975.

4. Allen, Jeffrey G., J.D., C.P.C., *Jeff Allen's Best: The Resume*. New York: John Wiley & Sons, 1990.

5. Allen, *Surviving Corporate Downsizing.*, pp. 68–69.

6. *Ibid.*, pp. 69–70.

7. Molloy, John T., *John T. Molloy's New Dress for Success*. New York: Warner Books, 1988.

8. Molloy, John T., *The Woman's Dress for Success Book*. New York: Warner Books, 1978.

9. Allen, *How to Turn an Interview into a Job*, p. 26.

10. *Ibid.*, p. 27.

11. Maltz, Maxwell, M.D., F.I.C.S., *Psycho-Cybernetics*. New York: Pocket Books, 1969.

12. Allen, *How to Turn an Interview into a Job*, p. 22–25.

13. Allen, Jeffrey G., J.D., C.P.C., and Jess Gorkin, *Finding the Right Job at Midlife*. New York: Simon & Schuster, 1985, pp. 70–71.

14. *Ibid.*, pp. 72–75.

15. Dawson, Kenneth M., and Sheryl N. Dawson, *Job Search: The Total System*. New York: John Wiley & Sons, 1988, pp. 79–80.

16. Allen and Gorkin, *Finding the Right Job at Midlife*, pp. 104–105.

17. Allen, *Surviving Corporate Downsizing*, pp. 38–39.

18. *Ibid.*, pp. 49–51.

19. *Ibid.*, pp. 47–49.

20. *Ibid.*, p. 47.

21. Dawson and Dawson, *Job Search: The Total System*, pp. 89–93.

22. Allen, Jeffrey G., J.D., C.P.C., *The Perfect Job Reference*. New York: John Wiley & Sons, 1990, p. 3.

23. *Ibid.*, pp. 31–32.

24. *Ibid.*, pp. 23–24.

25. *Ibid.*, p. 42.

26. *Ibid.*, pp. 54–58.

27. *Ibid.*, pp. 63–68.

28. *Ibid.*, pp. 33–34.

29. Beatty, Richard H., *The Perfect Cover Letter*. (New York: John Wiley & Sons, 1989, p. 15.

30. Allen, *The Perfect Job Reference*, p. 73.

31. *Ibid.*, pp. 74–75.

32. *Ibid.*, p. 90.

33. *Ibid.*, p. 122.

34. *Ibid.*, p. 106.

35. *Ibid.*, p. 107.

36. *Ibid.*, p. 109.

37. *Ibid.*, pp. 111–112

38. Allen, *How to Turn an Interview into a Job*, pp. 87–90.

39. Eyler, David, *The Executive Moonlighter*. New York: John Wiley & Sons, 1989, pp. 112–114.

40. Allen, *Surviving Corporate Downsizing*, pp. 107–108.

41. *Ibid.*, pp. 102–103.

42. Bostwick, Burdette E., *111 Proven Techniques and Strategies for Getting the Job Interview*. New York: John Wiley & Sons, 1981, p. 125.

43. Eyler, *The Executive Moonlighter*, pp. 1–2.

Bibliography

Allen, Jeffrey G., J.D., C.P.C., and Jess Gorkin, *Finding the Right Job at Midlife*. New York: Simon & Schuster, 1985.

Allen, Jeffrey G., J.D. C.P.C., *How to Turn an Interview into a Job*. New York: Simon & Schuster, 1981.

Allen, Jeffrey G., J.D., C.P.C., *Jeff Allen's Best: The Resume*. New York: John Wiley & Sons, 1990.

Allen, Jeffrey G., J.D., C.P.C., *Jeff Allen's Best: Win the Job*. New York: John Wiley & Sons, 1990.

Allen, Jeffrey G., J.D., C.P.C., *The Perfect Job Reference*. New York: John Wiley & Sons, 1990.

Allen, Jeffrey G., J.D., C.P.C., *Surviving Corporate Downsizing*. New York: John Wiley & Sons, 1988.

Beatty, Richard H., *The Perfect Cover Letter*. New York: John Wiley & Sons, 1989.

Bostwick, Burdette E., *111 Proven Techniques and Strategies for Getting the Job Interview*. New York: John Wiley & Sons, 1981.

Dawson, Kenneth M., and Sheryl N. Dawson, *Job Search: The Total System*. New York: John Wiley & Sons, 1988.

Eyler, David, *The Executive Moonlighter*. New York: John Wiley & Sons, 1989.

Korda, Michael, *Power! How to Get It, How to Use It*. New York: Ballantine Books, 1975.

Maltz, Maxwell, M.D., F.I.C.S., *Psycho-Cybernetics*. New York: Pocket Books, 1969.

Molloy, John T., *John T. Molloy's New Dress for Success*. New York: Warner Books, 1988.

Molloy, John T., *The Woman's Dress for Success Book*. New York: Warner Books, 1978.

Index

DATE DUE			
RESERVE			

Allen   230250